Barnes Fair
12·7·97

AN AMERICAN ODYSSEY

ELIA KAZAN

This book is dedicated to the memory of my wife
Jeannine, who helped me to organize it
(and did most of the translation)

Michel Ciment

DIRECTOR:

ELIA KAZAN

TITLE:

AN AMERICAN ODYSSEY

EDITED BY:

MICHEL CIMENT

BLOOMSBURY

First published in the English language 1988
Copyright © 1988 by Elia Kazan
English translation of 'Elia Kazan at the Crossroads'
by Michel Ciment © 1988 by Bloomsbury Publishing Ltd
Originally published as *Une Odyssée*
Américaine in 1987 by Calmann-Lévy,
© Calmann-Lévy 1987

Bloomsbury Publishing Ltd, 2 Soho Square, London W1V 5DE

British Library Cataloguing in Publication Data

Kazan, Elia, *1909* –
    An American odyssey.
    1. Cinema films. Directing
    I. Title
    791.43′0233

ISBN 0-7475-0241-2

Michel Ciment's introduction,
'Elia Kazan at the Crossroads',
was translated from
the French by Sally Sampson.

Printed in Great Britain
by Butler & Tanner Ltd,
Frome and London

CONTENTS

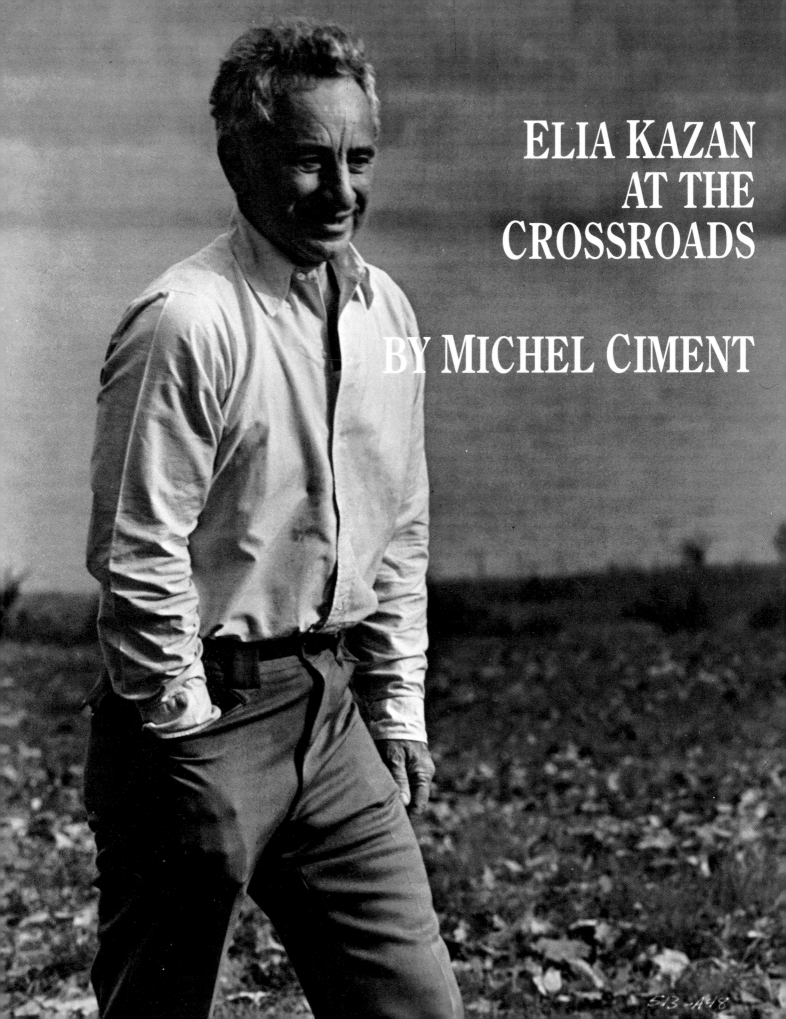

ELIA KAZAN
AT THE
CROSSROADS

BY MICHEL CIMENT

There are not many American film-makers who can express themselves about their art and combine action with thought. Elia Kazan is one of these rare beings. Working notes, letters to his collaborators, newspaper articles, lectures, prefaces: all are proofs of a constant desire to take stock of his working methods at various moments of his life. From this mass of material we have chosen what we feel to be the most important texts, to which Elia Kazan has kindly added some unpublished notes specially written for this book.

The reader will appreciate the interest of this collection. A creative artist with many faces, Kazan has been by turns, and sometimes simultaneously, actor, theatrical director, film-maker, founder of and teacher at the Actors' Studio, journalist and novelist. His artistic activity covers a period of nearly sixty years.

Moreover, his life led to his sharing in some of the great movements that shook twentieth-century America. A Greek of Anatolian origin, born in Istanbul, he was an immigrant at the age of four, then grew up in the heart of an ethnic minority in New York. Member of the Group Theatre in the 1930s, he was part of the intense artistic and political activity that marked out that decade, from the Great Crash to the New Deal. This youthful commitment – this fiercely critical way of looking at his country that would never leave him – undoubtedly explains his desire to analyse his own work in the same way as his contemporary, Orson Welles, another notable outsider among transatlantic film-makers.

In the early 1950s, Kazan went through one of the third major testing periods of his country's history, the McCarthy witch hunts. His evidence before the Committee for Un-American activities, his oaths of allegiance and his clearly expressed willingness to "name names" found an echo in his later work.

This work, and the journey through the century which it represents, is the "odyssey" which it is this book's chief purpose to illuminate. For Kazan is one of a small band of American directors whose films bear witness to a tireless striving to break new boundaries.

At the crossroads of the old Hollywood cinema and the "new wave" of the 1960s and 1970s, today his work stands out as a shining example. At a time when there is much talk about *auteur* cinema, here is a career which shows the slow progression of a film director from regular employment in a studio (the Fox period, 1944–50), to the development of more personal themes (*Viva Zapata!*, *On the Waterfront*), on to the production of his own films (starting with *East of Eden* in 1954) and finally to the writing of his own screenplays (*America America*, *The Arrangement*). His work is of pivotal importance in the formation of an industry which evolved from the domination of the big film companies to the independent productions of today.

His work is also a key pointer to a period when film-makers were more and more expressing doubts about America, after decades when most films reflected a confidence in the values of that society. Like Welles or Losey, Kazan is a child of the 1930s. He lived through that historical crisis – the Great Depression – after which nothing would ever be the same again. He re-examined official optimism, and made sure that social criticism would be marked by uncertainty and doubt.

Elia Kazan in 1969.

The film generation which is nearly contemporary with Kazan and includes Robert Aldrich, Richard Brooks, Nicholas Ray; then the directors who came from television (John Frankenheimer, Robert Mulligan, Arthur Penn); and finally the so-called American New Wave all owe a debt, frequently acknowledged, sometimes hidden or unconscious, to films where the crisis of a society searching for its own identity found expression. This crisis was experienced by the characters played by the actors shaped by the Method School of acting. The Actors' Studio, forcing the actor to concentrate, to achieve a state of "public solitude", to develop an emotional and sensory memory, was an ideal school for giving life to parts rich in conflicting tensions at the heart of relationships in love, family or social life.

This exploration of the unconscious – of the "inner I" – fitted perfectly into an era (the end of the 1940s) which was discovering psychoanalysis, and to which the work of Tennessee Williams bears witness. The influence of Freud, combined with the social ideas which had shaped Kazan in his youth, gave a double aspect to his richest films. "To change the world" and "to change people's lives" – these two key ideas, which led to the great cataclysms of our times heralded by Marx and Freud, can be summed up, for every genuine artist who won't resort to subterfuge, in a simple question: what gets in the way of change, in life and in the world? In this respect, *Splendor in the Grass* is a lucid analysis of all the pressures that bear down on the individual: it shows how social and economic structures are inextricably linked with psychological inhibitions and end by destroying others. The germ of this idea was present in *Baby Doll*, and it was to become central to his work. Another pivotal theme takes us back through time, for Kazan's films are a voyage of discovery both of the characters in them and of America herself. *America America*, a film about emigration, describes the birth of a man at the same time as the birth of a nation. *East of Eden* shows the battle of the generations against a backdrop of land speculation. *Splendor in the Grass* evokes the crash of 1929, and *Wild River* the experience of the New Deal and the Tennessee Valley Authority. In showing trade union corruption (*On the Waterfront*), the links between television, advertising and politics (*A Face in the Crowd*), the sham hypocrisy of the consumer society (*The Arrangement*) or the effects of the Vietnam War (*The Visitors*), Kazan chose the most topical subjects – but with him the present and the past are indissolubly linked. In this sense his art is above all temporal, even in its very excesses – the extended length and the moments of sharp tension. His subject is the passage of time: the way that time transforms and erodes human beings and things, the conflict between the old and the new. His films feed on contradictions – hence their rejection of Manicheism, and the questions that they ask tirelessly: the need to find one's roots and at the same time to burn one's house down; the desire to hide in the womb of the old family home and the painful realization that it is time to leave, that, whatever you do, "you can't go home again."

In his films, we see America transform herself, and undergo sea changes, and with her these stubborn, wilful, tortured, frustrated characters who draw their strength from adversity, as in the lines from Wordsworth quoted by the heroine of *Splendor in the Grass*: "We will grieve not, rather find/Strength in what remains behind." In this cinema of doubt and frustrated violence, and romantic indecision, we also find a love of the organic, of the physical, of all things that grow, then perish. A film-maker of contradiction, then. A film-maker torn by conflicting aspirations, a film-maker of suspicion and imperfection – that is, a truly modern artist at a time when beliefs are questioned and man is examining his soul. Kazan is a materialist, physically in love with the world as if with a woman's body: he's also a Dostoevskyan who believes that man always pays for what he has done, and that guilt will always pursue him. An artist who likes to teach, he's also a poet searching for contemplation and simplicity. In his fast-moving films, there are few calm moments. Full of dissonance and swirling eddies of feeling, they are still striving for a higher kind of harmony. Stylizing reality, they nevertheless point the way towards realism. A proud, deeply personal film-maker, Kazan is still able to orchestrate the kind of teamwork in which directors of photography, distinguished writers, famous actors whom he has often trained himself, manage to give of their best without sacrificing their individuality, integrating themselves into a coherent and productive whole.

With his living contradictions, Kazan is a director who is always in movement, spurning ready-made solutions and the status quo, whether moral or aesthetic. Conservative and progressive at one and the same time, it's hardly surprising that he unsettles people, and provokes the most extreme reactions. What so many young film-makers, actors and critics have recognized in him is an echo of their own dissatisfaction, their own conditioning. And the attraction that his films still exert on a wide public must be because they have never dated.

Witnesses to this are Terrence Malik, who, in *Badlands* and *Days of Heaven*, harks back to James Dean and *East of Eden*; Martin Scorsese, who ended *Raging Bull* with a pastiche of the famous scene between Rod Steiger and Marlon Brando in *On the Waterfront*; Francis Coppola, who evokes *America America* in *The Godfather, Part Two*; and James Toback, whose *Fingers*, through Harvey Keitel, is an act of homage to the Method. This actor, like Robert De Niro, Al Pacino, Jack Nicholson or Dustin Hoffman, owes much to the man who revolutionized the actor's work during the 1950s. And, since then, there could hardly be a more revealing film than the misunderstood and underestimated *The Last Tycoon*: an *auteur* film under the disguise of a super-production conceived by Sam Spiegel; a homage to – and criticism of – the golden days of Hollywood; a romantic film, veined with romanticism, but edged with a steely disillusioned realism. A film which brings together all the different forces and tendencies that fed Hollywood over forty years: Fitzgerald, of course, revisited by Pinter, the foreigner, but also Spiegel, the "old hands" Robert Mitchum, Tony Curtis and Ray Milland, and the new hands, Robert De Niro and Jack Nicholson. And Kazan himself, at the crossroads where all paths meet. Kazan, whose twentieth film – ten years after *The Last Tycoon* – we are awaiting, which will continue the semi-auto-biographical quest which *America America* began.

FILM DIRECTOR

ALL YOU
NEED TO KNOW, KIDS

Text of a lecture given to the students of Wesleyan University, which had just run an Elia Kazan retrospective (autumn 1972).

This is the traditional instant for me to thank all of you who have helped mount this retrospective. I think you did a damned good job. Together we may have finally begun to move this university, and, by influence, those like it, towards a serious and devoted study of films as the art of this day. I hope and – judging by the number of you here present – have begun to believe that this retrospective and the appearance of a distinguished French critic on your campus will be the first of a series of similar events.

A reporter from your campus paper, the *Argus*, asked me why I'd given my papers to this university. I gave a superficial answer. I said Wesleyan is close to where I live, so my things would be available to me after an hour's drive. I added that the authorities here had been generous, eager and accommodating. All true.

But the real reason was that for years I've been thinking it was about time our institutions of learning became involved in film as the subject of formal courses of study both for themselves as pieces of art and for what they say as witnesses to their day. I saw an opportunity here to progress this cause.

Tonight I urge you to direct the program of this university to now place the movie on the same basis of regard, esteem and concern as – for instance – the novel.

We simply can no longer think of movies in the way we used to years ago, as a pastime between supper and bed. What your faculty has particularly contributed here was to make these two weeks of study with Michel Ciment part of the curriculum. Credit towards graduation was given, a first step in the right direction.

I have been examining the excellent book[1] you have assembled with this showing of my work – I was going to say life's work, but that would not be totally accurate. It should be noted that at the Yale Drama School and elsewhere I had a valuable time as a backstage technician. I was a stage carpenter and I lit shows. Then there was a

Overleaf: Elia Kazan (*left*) with his director of photography, Joe MacDonald, during the shooting of *Pinky* (1949).

Elia Kazan (*left*) with director of photography, Ralph Steiner, during the shooting of *The People of the Cumberland* (1937).

tedious time as a radio actor, playing hoodlums for bread. I had a particularly educational four years as a stage manager helping and watching directors and learning a great deal. And, in between, I had a lively career as a stage actor in some good plays. All these activities were very valuable to me.

In time, I was fortunate enough to have directed the works of the best dramatists of a couple of the decades which have now become history. I was privileged to serve Williams, Miller, Bill Inge, Archie MacLeish, Sam Behrman and Bob Anderson and put some of their plays on the stage. I thought of my role with these men as that of a craftsman who tried to realize as well as he could the author's intentions in the author's vocabulary and within his range, style and purpose.

I have not thought of my film work that way.

Some of you may have heard of the *auteur* theory. That concept is partly a critic's plaything. Something for them to spat over and use to fill a column. But it has its point, and that point is simply that the director is the true author of the film. The director TELLS the film, using a vocabulary the lesser part of which is an arrangement of words.

A screenplay's worth has to be measured less by its language than by its architecture and how that dramatizes the theme. A screenplay, we directors soon enough learn, is not a piece of writing as much as it is a construction. We learn to feel for the skeleton under the skin of words.

Meyerhold, the great Russian stage director, said that words were the decoration on the skirts of action. He was talking about theatre but I've always thought his observation applied more aptly to film.

It occurred to me when I was considering what to say here that since you all don't see directors – it's unique for Wesleyan to have a film-maker standing where I am after a showing of his work, while you have novelists, historians, poets and writers of various kinds of studies living among you – that it might be fun if I were to try to list for you and for my own sport what a film director needs to know as well as what personal characteristics and attributes he might advantageously possess.

How must he educate himself?
Of what skills is his craft made?
What kind of a man must he be?

Of course I'm talking about a book-length subject. Stay easy, I'm not going to read a book to you tonight. I will merely try to list the fields of knowledge necessary to him, and later those personal qualities he might happily possess, give them to you as one might chapter headings, section leads, first sentences of paragraphs, without elaboration.

Here we go.

Literature. Of course. All periods, all languages, all forms. Naturally a film director is better equipped if he's well read. Jack Ford, who introduced himself with the words, "I make Westerns", was an extremely well and widely read man.

The literature of the theatre. For one thing, so the film director will appreciate the difference from film. He should also study the classic theatre literature for construction, for exposition of theme, for the means of characterization, for dramatic poetry, for the elements of unity, especially that unity created by pointing to climax and then for climax as the essential and final embodiment of the theme.

The craft of screen dramaturgy. Every director, even in those rare instances when he doesn't work with a writer or two – Fellini works with a squadron – must take responsibility for the screenplay. He has not only to guide rewriting but to eliminate what's unnecessary, cover faults, appreciate non-verbal possibilities, ensure correct structure, have a sense of screen time,

[1]*Working With Kazan*, an illustrated filmography (Wesleyan University Press, 1972).

With Melvyn Douglas and
Katharine Hepburn, during
the shooting of *The Sea of
Grass* (1946).

Elia Kazan (*right*) during
the shooting of *Boomerang*
(1946).

16

how much will elapse, in what places, for what purposes. Robert Frost's *Tell Everything a Little Faster* applies to all expositional parts. In the climaxes time is unrealistically extended, "stretched", usually by close-ups.

The film director knows that beneath the surface of his screenplay there is a subtext, a calendar of intentions and feelings and inner events. What appears to be happening, he soon learns, is rarely what is happening. This subtext is one of the film director's most valuable tools. It is what he directs. You will rarely see a veteran director holding a script as he works – or even looking at it. Beginners yes.

Most directors' goal today is to write their own scripts. But that is our oldest tradition. Chaplin would hear that Griffith Park had been flooded by a heavy rainfall. Packing his crew, his stand-by actors and his equipment in a few cars, he would rush there, making up the story of the two-reel comedy *en route*, the details on the spot.

The director of films should know comedy as well as drama. Jack Ford used to call most parts "comics". He meant, I suppose, a way of looking at people without false sentiment, through an objectivity that deflated false heroics and undercut self-favoring and finally revealed a saving humor in the most tense moments. The Human Comedy, another Frenchman called it. The fact that Billy Wilder is always amusing doesn't make his films less serious.

Quite simply the screen director must know either by training or by instinct how to feed a joke and how to score with it, how to anticipate and protect laughs. He might well study Chaplin and the other great two-reel comedy-makers for what are called sight gags, non-verbal laughs, amusement derived from "business", stunts and moves, and simply from funny faces and odd bodies. This vulgar foundation – the banana peel and the custard pie – are basic to our craft and part of its health. Wyler and

Stevens began by making two-reel comedies and I seem to remember Capra did, too.

American film directors would do well to know our vaudeville traditions. Just as Fellini adored the clowns, music hall performers and the circuses of his country and paid them homage again and again in his work, our film-maker would do well to study magic. I believe some of the wonderful cuts in *Citizen Kane* came from the fact that Welles was a practising magician and so understood the drama of sudden unexpected appearances and the startling change. Think, too, of Bergman, how often he uses magicians and sleight of hand.

The director should know opera, its effects and its absurdities, a subject in which Bernard Bertolucci is schooled. He should know the American musical stage and its tradition, but even more important, the great American musical films. He must not look down on these; we love them for very good reasons.

Our man should know acrobatics, the art of juggling and tumbling, the techniques of the wry comic song. The techniques of the Commedia dell'Arte are used, it seems to me, in a film called *O Lucky Man!* Lindsay Anderson's master, Bertolt Brecht, adored the Berlin satirical cabaret of his time and adapted their techniques.

With Ethel Barrymore during the shooting of *Pinky* (1949).

Let's move faster because it's endless. Painting and sculpture, their history, their revolutions and counter-revolutions. The painters of the Italian Renaissance used their mistresses as models for the Madonna, so who can blame a film director for using his girl friend in a leading role – unless she does a bad job.

Many painters have worked in the theatre. Bakst, Picasso, Aronson and Matisse come to mind. More will. Here, we are still with Disney.

Which brings us to dance. In my opinion it's a considerable asset if the director's knowledge here is not only theoretical but prac-

The film director must know music, classic, so called – too much of an umbrella word, that! Let us say of all periods. And as with sculpture and painting, he must know what social situations and currents the music came out of.

Of course he must be particularly INTO the music of his own day, acid rock, Latin rock, blues and jazz, pop, tin pan alley, barbershop, corn, country, Chicago, New Orleans, Nashville.

The film director should know the history of stage scenery, its development from background to environment and so to the settings INSIDE which films are played

(Right) With Karl Malden, the producer David Weisbart (back view) and Vivien Leigh, during the shooting of A Streetcar Named Desire (1950).

tical and personal. Dance is an essential part of a screen director's education. It's a great advantage for him if he can "move". It will help him not only to move actors but move the camera. The film director, ideally, should be able as a choreographer, quite literally so. I don't mean the tango in Bertolucci's last or the high school gym dance in American Graffiti as much as I do the battle scenes in D. W. Griffith's Birth of a Nation which are pure choreography and very beautiful. Look at Ford's cavalry charges that way. Or Jim Cagney's dance of death on the long steps in The Roaring Twenties.

out. Notice I stress INSIDE WHICH as opposed to IN FRONT OF. The construction of scenery for film-making was traditionally the work of architects. The film director must study from life, from newspaper clippings and from his own photographs, dramatic environments and particularly how they affect behavior.

I recommend to every young director that he start his own collection of clippings and photographs and, if he's able, his own sketches.

(Left) Shooting Panic in the Streets.

The film director must know costuming, its history through all periods, its techniques and what it can be as expression. Again, life is a prime source. We learn to study, as we enter each place, each room, how the people there have chosen to present themselves. "How he comes on," we say.

Costuming in films is so expressive a means that it is inevitably the basic choice of the director. Visconti is brilliant here. So is Bergman in a more modest vein. The best way to study this again is to notice how people dress as an expression of what they wish to gain from any occasion, what their intention is. Study your husband, study your wife, how their attire is an expression of each day's mood and hope, their good days, their days of low confidence, their time of stress and how it shows in clothing.

Lighting. Of course. The various natural effects, the cross light of morning, the heavy flat top light of midday – avoid it except for an effect – the magic hour, so called by cameramen, dusk. How do they affect mood? Obvious. We know it in life. How do they affect behavior? Study that. Five o'clock is a low time, let's have a drink! Directors choose the time of day for certain scenes with these expressive values in mind. The master here is Jack Ford, who used to plan his shots within a sequence to best use certain natural effects that he could not create but could very advantageously wait for.

Colors? Their psychological effect. So obvious I will not expand. Favorite colors. Faded colors. The living grays. In *Baby Doll* you saw a master cameraman – Boris Kaufman – making great use of white on white, to help describe the washed-out Southern whites.

And, of course, there are the instruments which catch all and should dramatize all; the tools the director speaks through, the CAMERA and the TAPE RECORDER. The film director obviously must know the camera and its lenses, which lens creates which effect, which one lies, which one

Elia Kazan (*right*) and Marlon Brando (*left*) during the shooting of *Viva Zapata!* (1951).

20

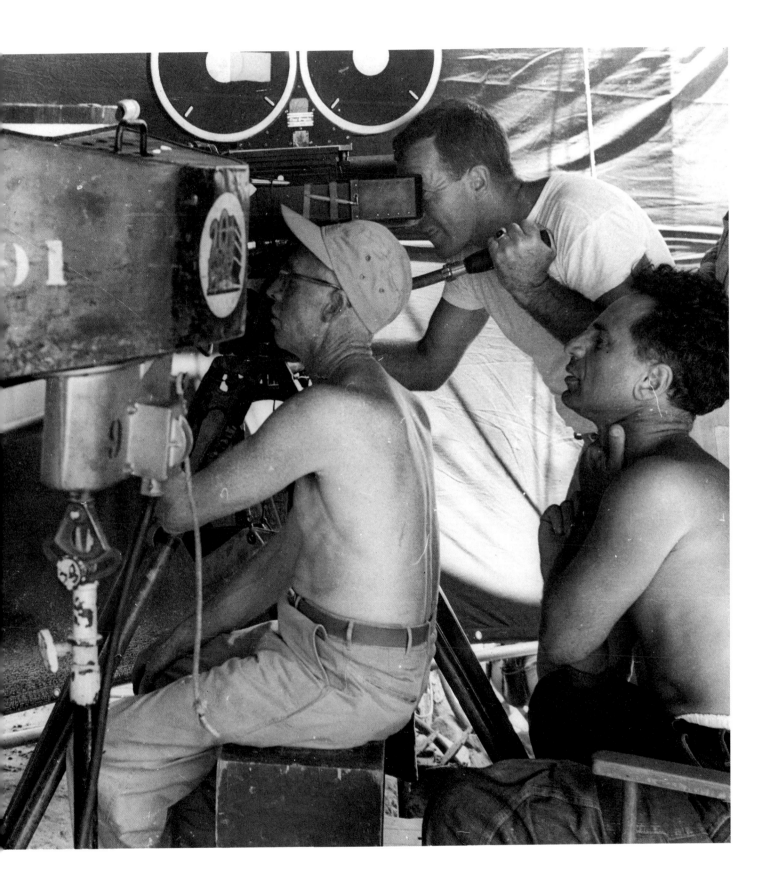

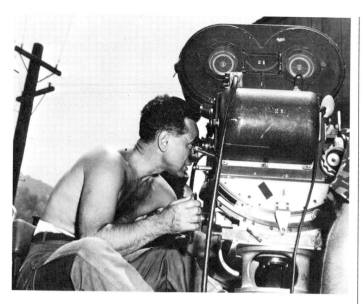

Shooting *East of Eden* (1954).

tells the cruel truth. Which filters bring out the clouds. The director must know the various speeds at which the camera can roll and especially the effects of small variations in speed. He must also know the various camera mountings, the cranes and the dollies and the possible moves he can make, the configurations in space through which he can pass this instrument. He must know the zoom well enough so he won't use it – or almost never.

He should be intimately acquainted with the tape recorder. Andy Warhol carries one everywhere he goes. Practice "bugging" yourself and your friends. Notice how often speech overlaps.

The film director must understand the weather, how it's made and where, how it moves, its warning signs, its crises, the kind of clouds and what they mean. Remember the clouds in *Shane*. He must know weather as dramatic expression, be on the alert to capitalize on changes in weather as one of his means. He must study how heat and cold, rain and snow, a soft breeze, driving wind affect people and whether it's true that there are more expressions of group rage during a long hot summer and why.

The film director should know the city, ancient and modern, but particularly his city, the one he loves like DeSica loves Naples, Fellini Rimini, Bergman his island, Ray Calcutta, Renoir the French countryside, Clair the city of Paris. His city, its features, its operation, its substructure, its scenes behind the scenes, its functionaries, its police, fire-fighters, garbage collectors, post office workers, commuters and what they ride, its cathedrals and its whore houses.

The film director must know the country – no, that's too general a term. He must know the mountains and the plains, the deserts of our great south-west, the heavy oily bottom-soil of the Delta, the hills of New England. He must know the water off Marblehead and Old Orchard Beach, too cold for lingering and the water off the Florida Keys which invites dawdling. Again these are means of expression that he has and among them he must make his choices. He must know how a breeze from a fan can animate a dead-looking set by stirring a curtain.

He must know the sea, first-hand, chance a shipwreck so he'll appreciate its power. He must know under the surface of the sea; it may occur to him, if he does, to play a scene there. He must have crossed our rivers and know the strength of their currents. He must have swum in our lakes and caught fish in our streams. You think I'm exaggerating. Why did old man Flaherty and his Mrs spend at least a year in an environment before they exposed a foot of negative? While you're young, you aspiring directors, hitch-hike our country!

And topography, the various trees, flowers, ground cover, grasses. And the sub-surface, shale, sand, gravel, New England ledge, six feet of old river bottom? What kind of man works each and how does it affect him?

Animals too. How they resemble human beings. How to direct a chicken to enter a room on cue. I had that problem once and I'm ashamed to tell you how I did it. What a

Polishing the script, on the set of *Wild River* (1960).

With Montgomery Clift and (*left of Kazan*) director of photography Ellsworth Fredericks, during the shooting of *Wild River* (1960).

cat might mean to a love scene. The symbolism of horses. The family life of the lion, how tender! The patience of a cow.

Of course the film director should know acting, its history and its techniques. The more he knows about acting, the more at ease he will be with actors. At one period of his growth, he should force himself on stage or before the camera so he knows this experientially, too. Some directors, and very famous ones, still fear actors instead of embracing them as comrades in a task. But, by contrast, there is the great Jean Renoir, see him in *Rules of the Game*. And his follower and lover, Truffaut in *The Wild Child*, now in *Day for Night*.

The director must know how to stimulate, even inspire the actor. Needless to say he must also know how to make an actor seem NOT to act. How to put him or her at their ease, bring them to that state of relaxation where their creative faculties are released.

The film director must understand the instrument known as the VOICE. He must also know SPEECH. And that they are not the same, as different as resonance and phrasing. He should also know the various regional accents of his country and what they tell about character.

All in all he must know enough in all these areas so his actors trust him completely. This is often achieved by giving the impression that any task he asks of them, he can perform, perhaps even better than they can. This may not be true, but it's not a bad impression to create.

The film director, of course, must be up on the psychology of behavior, "normal" and abnormal. He must know that they are linked, that one is often the extension or intensification of the other and that under certain stresses which the director will create within a scene as it's acted out, one kind of behavior can be seen becoming the other. And that is drama.

The film director must be prepared by knowledge and training to handle neurotics. Why? Because most actors are. Perhaps all. What makes it doubly interesting is that the film director often is. Stanley Kubrick won't get on a plane – well, maybe that isn't so neurotic. But we are all delicately balanced – isn't that a nice way to put it? Answer this: how many interesting people have you met who are not – a little?

Of course we work with the psychology of the audience. We know it differs from that of its individual members. In cutting films great comedy directors like Hawks and Preston Sturges allow for the group reactions they expect from the audience, they play on these. Hitchcock has made this his art.

The film director must be learned in the erotic arts. The best way here is through personal experience. But there is a history here, an artistic technique. Pornography is not looked down upon. The film director will admit to a natural interest in how other people do it. Boredom, cruelty, banality are the only sins. Our man, for instance, might study the Chinese erotic prints and those scenes on Greek vases of the Golden Age which museum curators hide.

Of course the film director must be an authority, even an expert on the various attitudes of love-making, the postures and intertwinings of the parts of the body, the expressive parts and those generally considered less expressive. He may well have, like Buñuel with feet, special fetishes. He is not concerned to hide these, rather he will probably express his inclinations with relish.

The director, here, may come to believe that suggestion is more erotic than show. Then study how to go about it.

Then there is war. Its weapons, its techniques, its machinery, its tactics, its history – oh my –

Where is the time to learn all this?

On the set of *Splendor in the Grass* (1960).

Overleaf: Elia Kazan (*far left*) during the shooting of *America America* (1964).

Do not think, as you were brought up to think, that education starts at six and stops at twenty-one, that we learn only from teachers, books and classes. For us that is the least of it. The life of a film director is a totality and he learns as he lives. Everything is pertinent, there is nothing irrelevant or trivial. *O Lucky Man*, to have such a profession! Every experience leaves its residue of knowledge behind. Every book we read applies to us. Everything we see and hear, if we like it, we steal it. Nothing is irrelevant. It all belongs to us.

So history becomes a living subject, full of dramatic characters, not a bore about treaties and battles. Religion is fascinating as a kind of poetry expressing fear and loneliness and hope. The film director reads *The Golden Bough* because sympathetic magic and superstition interest him, these beliefs of the ancients and the savages parallel those of his own time's people. He studies ritual because ritual as a source of stage and screen *mise en scène* is an increasingly important source.

Economics a bore? Not to us. Consider the demoralization of people in a labor pool, the panic in currency, the reliance of a nation on imports and the leverage this gives the country supplying the needed imports. All these affect or can affect the characters and milieux with which our film is concerned. Consider the facts behind the drama of *On the Waterfront*. Wonder how we could have shown more of them.

The film director doesn't just eat. He studies food. He knows the meals of all nations and how they're served, how consumed, what the variations of taste are, the effect of the food, food as a soporific, food as an aphrodisiac, as a means of expression of character. Remember the scene in *Tom Jones*? *La Grande Bouffe*?

And, of course, the film director tries to keep up with the flow of life around him, the contemporary issues, who's pressuring who, who's winning, who's losing, how pressure shows in the politician's body and

face and gestures. Inevitably, the director will be a visitor at night court. And he will not duck jury duty. He studies advertising and goes to "product meetings" and spies on those who make the ads that influence people. He watches talk shows and marvels how Jackie Susann peddles it. He keeps up on the moves, as near as he can read them, of the secret underground societies. And skyjacking, what's the solution? He talks to pilots. It's a perfect drama – that situation – no exit.

Travel. Yes. As much as he can. Let's not get into that.

With Kirk Douglas (*far left*) during the shooting of *The Arrangement* (1969).

I've undoubtedly left out a great number of things and what I've left out is significant, no doubt, and describes some of my own shortcomings.

Oh! Of course. I've left out the most important thing. The subject the film director must know most about, know best of all, see in the greatest detail and in the most pitiless light with the greatest appreciation of the ambivalences at play is – what?

Right. Himself.

There is something of himself, after all, in every character he properly creates. He understands people truly through understanding himself truly.

The silent confessions he makes to himself are the greatest source of wisdom he has. And of tolerance for others. And for love, even that. There is the admission of hatred to awareness and its relief through understanding and a kind of resolution in brotherhood.

What kind of a person must a film director train himself to be?

What qualities does he need? Here are a few. Those of –

A white hunter leading a safari into dangerous and unknown country.

A construction gang foreman, who knows his physical problems and their solutions and is ready, therefore, to insist on these solutions.

A psychoanalyst who keeps a patient functioning despite intolerable tensions and stresses, both professional and personal.

A hypnotist who works with the unconscious to achieve his ends.

A poet, a poet of the camera, able both to capture the decisive moment of Cartier-Bresson or to wait all day like Paul Strand for a single shot which he makes with a bulky camera fixed on a tripod.

An outfielder for his legs. The director stands much of the day, dares not get tired, so he has strong legs. Think back and remember how the old-time directors dramatized themselves. By puttees, right.

Sports? The best directed shows on TV today are the professional football games. Why? Study them. You are shown not only the game from far and middle distance and close-up, you are shown the bench, the way the two coaches sweat it out, the rejected sub, Craig Morton, waiting for Staubach to be hurt and Woodall, does he really like Namath? Johnson, Snead? Watch the spectators, too. Think how you might direct certain scenes playing with a ball, or swimming or sailing – even though that is nowhere indicated in the script. Or watch a ball game like Hepburn and Tracy in George Stevens's film, *Woman of the Year*!

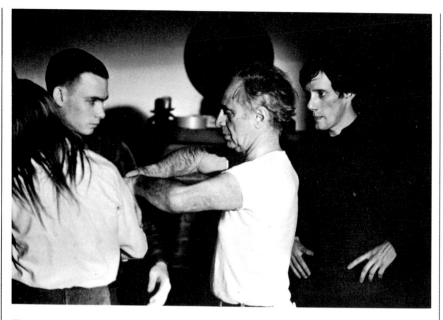

With Patricia Joyce, Steve Railsback and James Woods, during the shooting of *The Visitors* (1971).

The cunning of a trader in a Baghdad bazaar.

The firmness of an animal trainer. Obvious. Tigers!

A great host. At a sign from him, fine food and heart-warming drink appear.

The authority and sternness of her husband, the father who forgives nothing, expects obedience without question, brooks no nonsense.

The kindness of an old-fashioned mother who forgives all.

These alternatively.

The illusiveness of a jewel thief – no explanation, take my word for this one.

The blarney of a PR man, especially useful when the director is out in a strange and hostile location as I have many times been.

A very thick skin.

A very sensitive soul.

Simultaneously.

The patience, the persistence, the fortitude of a saint, the appreciation of pain, a taste for self-sacrifice, everything for the cause.

Cheeriness, jokes, playfulness, alternating with sternness, unwavering firmness. Pure doggedness.

An unwavering refusal to take less than he thinks right out of a scene, a performer, a co-worker, a member of his staff, himself.

Direction, finally, is the exertion of your will over other people, disguise it, gentle it, but that is the hard fact.

Above all – COURAGE. Courage, said Winston Churchill, is the greatest virtue; it makes all the others possible.

One final thing. The ability to say, "I am wrong." Or "I was wrong." Not as easy as it sounds. But in many situations, these three words, honestly spoken, will save the day. They are the words, very often, that the actors struggling to give the director what he wants most need to hear from him. Those words, "I was wrong, let's try it another way," the ability to say them can be a life-saver.

The director must accept the blame for everything. If the script stinks, he should have worked harder with the writers or himself before shooting. If the actor fails, the director failed him! Or made a mistake in choosing him. If the camera work is uninspired, whose idea was it to engage that cameraman? Or choose those set-ups? Even a costume – after all the director passed on it. The settings. The music, even the goddamn ads, why didn't he yell louder if he didn't like them? The director was there, wasn't he? Yes, he was there! He's always there!

That's why he gets all that money, to stand there, on that mound, unprotected, letting everybody shoot at him and deflecting the mortal fire from all the others who work with him.

The other people who work on a film can hide.

They have the director to hide behind. And people deny the *auteur* theory!

After listening to me so patiently you have a perfect right now to ask, "Oh, come on, aren't you exaggerating to make some kind of point?"

Of course I'm exaggerating and it is to make a point.

But only a little exaggerating.

The fact is that a director from the moment a phone call gets him out of bed in the morning – "Rain today. What scene do you want to shoot?" – until he escapes into the dark at the end of shooting to face, alone, the next day's problems, is called upon to answer an unrelenting string of questions, to make decision after decision in one after another of the fields I've listed. That's what a director is, the man with the answers.

Watch Truffaut playing Truffaut in *Day for Night*, watch him as he patiently, carefully, sometimes thoughtfully, other times very quickly, answers questions. You will see better than I can tell you how these answers keep his film going. Truffaut has caught our life on the set perfectly.

Do things get easier and simpler as you get older and have accumulated some or all of this savvy?

Not at all. The opposite. The more a director knows, the more he's aware how many different ways there are to do every film, every scene.

And the more he has to face that final awful limitation, not of knowledge but of character. Which is what? The final limitation and the most terrible one is the limitation of his

own talent. You find, for instance, that you truly do have the faults of your virtues. And that limitation you can't do much about. Even if you have the time.

One last postscript. The director, that miserable son of a bitch, as often as not these days has to get out and promote the dollars and the pounds, scrounge for the liras, francs and marks, hock his family's home, his wife's jewels and his own future so he can make his film. This process of raising the wherewithal inevitably takes ten to a hundred times longer than making the film itself. But the director does it because he has to – who else will? Who else loves the film that much?

So, my friends, you've seen how much you have to know and what kind of a bastard you have to be. How hard you have to train yourself and in how many different ways. All of which I did. I've never stopped trying to educate myself and to improve myself.

So now pin me to the wall – this is your last chance. Ask me how with all that knowledge and all that wisdom, all that training and all those capabilities, including the strong legs of a major league outfielder, how did I manage to mess up some of the films I've directed so badly?

Ah, but that's the charm of it!

With Ingrid Boulting and Robert De Niro during the shooting of *The Last Tycoon* (1976).

FEEDBACK FROM AFAR

An article written for the 200th number of *Positif* (1977).

Now Bobby De Niro is our media pet and I believe he's strong enough to survive the attention. In a recent interview he gave *Time* he generously praised the directors with whom he'd worked and, in an added paragraph, said he liked working with me as well. I gave him, he said, the impression of a father who didn't quite approve of what

(*right*) Robert De Niro in
The Last Tycoon (1976).

his children were doing but loved them anyway.

Insults I don't answer. Praise I speak to. Especially kind words from a man I like as much as I do De Niro. Friendships in our culture rarely survive a financial failure. Ours did.

What Bobby said is true. I do love the generation coming up and, he's right again, I might say something critical about them.

They've seen too many movies.

That's OK for critics. But I don't think a director should see more than a movie a month. He should devote himself to more frivolous concerns: the theatre of the streets, the drama in his own home, forgiving his parents, fertilizing his love affairs, hedging his personal disasters, the cultivation of the widest circle of friends possible for him, travel.

And perhaps some reading. Enough history to cast the cool light of doubt over the men and events he studied in school.

In short his own life. His self.

It seems to me that too often the creative source of the new American films I see is another film. Or a number of other films, usually classics.

Classics are classics because they cannot be matched.

Have you noticed that most really creative people don't give a damn about the work of other artists in their field? Catch one of these fellows in a truth-telling mood, particularly the ones you admire most, and they'll tell you they couldn't care less what their brother artists are doing. When they seem to – your informant may confess – they're pretending.

I haven't seen working artists enjoying each other socially either. When they're dragged into the same room by a celebrity-struck hostess, they don't know what to say to each other and soon drift apart.

Still the impulse behind so many films made by our "new ones" is the director's wish he were more like someone else. Eisenstein, Welles, Hawks, Fellini, Bergman, Sturgess, Antonioni, Kurosawa – all those names the critics love to string together.

Homage! A craven word! Leave it, my young friends, to the men who mount retrospectives and manage festivals. Don't indulge those retrospectives, don't go to the festivals. Save all that till you're eighty.

A close friend of mine told me he found Peter Bogdanovitch, a man I've not met, to be arrogant. I don't think he's arrogant enough. Too many of his films are some kind of homage.

"I want to do a Western now." Have you heard that? "I want to do a forties musical." "A thirties gangster picture." "A big costume epic." "An American *Seven Samurai* or *Rashomon.*" "I will update *The Lady Eve.*" It's the era of the remake.

And the next thing you probably heard went something like this: "But it's not really a Western, it's about the inability to love." Or, "It's really not a Warner Brothers gangster film, it's about McCarthyism." Or, "It's really not a prison break picture, it's about a failure to communicate." And so on. And on.

Another thing. Why is it that so often when serious themes are attacked, the film takes the form of the Drama of the Falsely Accused?

For instance the hero is accused of being homosexual but really he is not; he turns out to be rather macho, in fact. Or he is accused of being a spy but he turns out to be the most patriotic one of us all and the truest. A murderer? Look again. The cop did it. A Communist? Don't be silly. All Communists brought before the corrupt American justice system were falsely accused.

Robert De Niro and Ingrid
Boulting in *The Last
Tycoon* (1976).

34

The real drama would be if the person accused was what he was accused of being. Then the issue might be explored and justice itself brought to trial.

One rarely sees a film where its author has recognized that there are always two sides to all important issues. That difficult decisions are difficult because whichever way a man goes, he loses something. That clarity is often over-simplification and over-simplification does not simplify, it muddies.

One reason is that this kind of view can only come to awareness when the film-maker has himself been on the horns of the issue he's handling. *When he's been there.*

With all too many of our good young film-makers, one feels, yes, they've been there, and where they've been is to the movies.

All art speaks the truth of a single eccentric, a kind of freak who has only one way of seeing the world around him, his own. Could Giacometti sculpt fat figures?

Someone said, "The only documentary anyone can make is a documentary about himself, what his eyes and his eyes alone see."

Yes, I do like the new young film-makers crowding up. But what I might say to them is, "While you're scrambling and climbing and giving voice, make sure it's your own voice."

Hommage à Hitch, *hommage à* Akira, *hommage à* Orson, *hommage à* Federico, *à* Buñuel, Renoir, Antonioni. By all means. But leave it to the festivalists, the critics and the people who collect autographs.

You, my friends, pay homage to yourselves.

DIRECTING IS THE GREATEST ART

Unpublished notes written at different periods.

Directing is like all arts: as you get better, it gets harder.

Don't give the audience the necessary exposition until you make them want the exposition. Cf. love-making. Don't just push it in before they're ready and eager for it.

A short letter to artists: the drama is happening right under your nose and you're looking elsewhere. Thornton Wilder said, "The daily life, the daily life, the daily life."

Sympathy must be wide. It's not a matter of getting the audience to love one of the characters; it's a matter of making them love all the characters.

I was called an actor's director. While I am proud of that, it also points to a lack that makes me uncomfortable. What's the matter with my camera work? Haskell Wexler[1] said I have no eye. True or not? I don't think so. But I do start from the actors. The first thing I do on the set in the morning is direct the scene with the actors. I have some idea of where I mean to put the camera but I don't tell anyone because I may change my mind.

I discovered an interesting thing when I first went to California in 1937. I thought that the most interesting contrast I would encounter there would be between the kind of acting I'd learned in the Group and that in the films of the old-time directors in the old Hollywood tradition. To my surprise I found that they had reacted negatively to the same kind of acting that had made the Group revolt artistically, the mannered, inflated, narcissistic techniques of the old theatre. The reaction of the old Hollywood directors to this was to say, "No acting, no acting!" Just say the lines. Be simple, cut the shit! Say the lines precisely as you have in all the other parts you've played. My camera will do the rest.

I spent a few months before undertaking my first picture watching how other directors worked with their actors. Not at all, is what I found. The moves were basic, simple and functional and were not related to whatever the scene might mean. Nothing was discussed with the actors. The cameraman and the director did have an understanding. The director believed that the actor he'd hired, and was paying a lot of money, knew his business. All he had to do, the director, was hold him down. And so on and on.

BASIC. The art of motion pictures is one of photographing looks not photographing dialogue. This means that in reaction scenes, thought scenes, back and forth internal inter-play scenes – stretch. Stretch the looks. Make the reactions of one character to another full length. (This is the opposite of what you do on stage where you tend to keep dialogue going.) In movies you exaggerate the length of the thinking and the stalls are worth more than the words. You photograph psychology. The motion-picture camera is a microscope. It is insight. It is insight. Literally. It goes into a person and reveals what the hell he is thinking. The key rule for directing dialogue and psychological scenes: find the internal events on each side and make the actors experience them and then really make them experience them in front of the camera and then photograph this experience close up. The camera reveals internal events that the eye would not notice, and the director connives in this insight.

Get love in your picture. I mean this simply. Photograph a man's love for his car. A tree's love for the sun. Man's love of an ideal. An emotion can be photographed. Like the fleck of the sea on a sunny day, a breeze can be photographed, a fish jumping can be photographed, love of life can be photographed. The camera is a medium for emotion. Pure emotion can be thus used too. But the key emotion that must be photographed is the key emotion of your

During the shooting of *America America* (1964).

[1] Director of photography of *America America*.

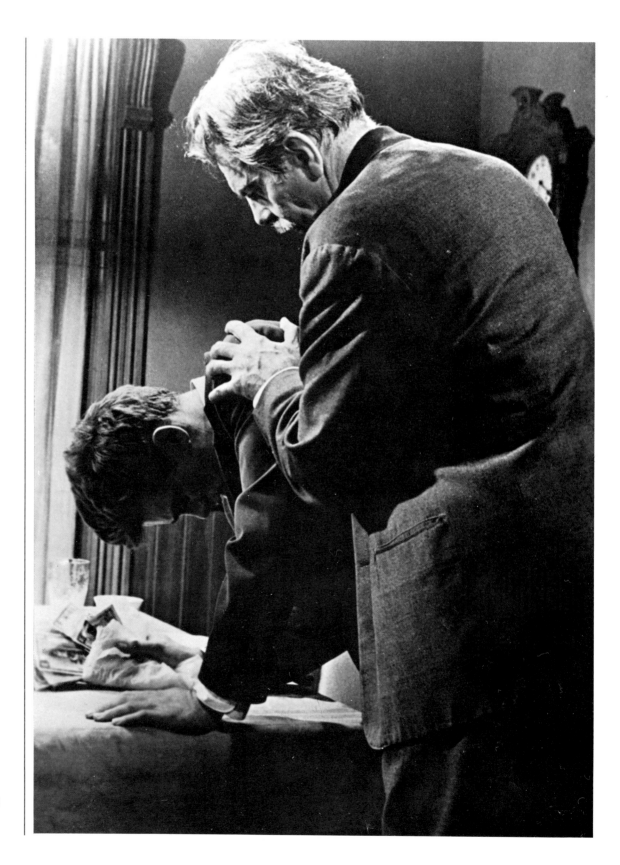

James Dean and Raymond
Massey in *East of Eden*
(1954).

Richard Davalos and James
Dean in *East of Eden*
(1954).

James Dean and Timothy Carey in *East of Eden* (1954).

piece: the love that puts the pain in conflict.

In every single angle back it up and go past the point where you expect (in your innocence) to be out of it. Determine an entrance and an exit, for instance. Carry it along as far as you can. Don't make things easy for yourself. Don't be obliging to yourself or the crew, or the cameraman, or whosoever. Get as much film on every angle as you possibly can. Also get into each angle as many possible cuts as you can. Later you will *desperately*, and I mean desperately, need little pieces of film. Don't forget the cutting room, brother, don't forget the cutting room.

And above all *don't be a nice guy*. Wyler: Toughest job a director has is to resist the temptation to be a nice guy. Don't let anyone hurry you. Don't be cooperative. Your biggest danger is your constant and unremitting anxiety to be liked. This is your enemy.

The end! The climax! This is where the *size* of the piece and of the film-maker is.

Here is where you must make a knot that you cannot get out of. The final strength and truth of a piece is in this: that you lead the audience into a really difficult situation – one from which there is no exit without mortal cost.

When you do your "thinking" on these things, consider the "finish". The kernel. The essence. The last five minutes where story and theme come together. Here is where you find out whether you have something or not. Whether you have something to say or not.

There is no real drama unless you have situations that push the main character to the extreme frontier of his nature. You must finally so arrange it that the leading character's back is to the wall. There he has no exit. He must face the music.

Don't let him off easy. (In *East of Eden* you let Dean off easy. Therefore the end is false!) You must never be able to ask the question: then what happens? What happens in a dramatic piece must be *final*! No exit.

Drama is the most dynamic of all arts. And the film strip, by its very nature – it runs! it is run! – is the most dynamic of the dramatic arts. You start a movement in the first feet that must gain momentum and charge till it crashes against an immovable wall in the last feet and that is it.

Sentimentality is the enemy of drama. It waters down the conflict. It is the sister of self-pity.

Last five minutes of *East of Eden*. Now you know that the old man would have died without a kind word for Dean – and that the kid would have to spend a long time climbing back.

Toughness fills an audience with the greatest of all theatre emotions – awe!

ABOUT SCREENWRITERS: BUDD SCHULBERG AND *A FACE IN THE CROWD*

1.

Preface to Budd Schulberg's screenplay for *A Face in the Crowd*, December 1956.

I arrived in Hollywood in 1944 to make my first motion picture, *A Tree Grows in Brooklyn*. I went from the train to the hotel and then checked in with my producer, Louis Lighton. He was a fine man, an old-timer, a fine producer, too. His eyesight was failing and I found him bent close over his desk peering through a very large magnifying glass. He was working on the script. He had before him Betty Smith's novel, as well as several earlier versions of the screenplay. These were being cannibalized – as they say at plane repair shops – in a search for usable parts. Laboriously and with practiced craftsmanship, the producer was putting the incidents together into sequences, arranging these for climax and shaping the whole into what he always called three "acts". Bud Lighton knew what he was doing; he'd done it since the days of the silents.

The screenplay was credited to Tess Slesinger and Frank Davis, but in all the nine months I was in Hollywood on this project, I never met these two people. Years later in New York, I heard of Miss Slesinger's death. I still hadn't met her. Another few years passed and one night at a party a strange man came up and introduced himself. It was Frank Davis.

I was fresh from the theatre and this separation of the writers from the director – and from their own work – came as a shock to me. I was to learn that it was regular practice.

I remember my first day at lunch in the Twentieth-Century Fox commissary. Behind the closed doors of the executive-dining room, I was told that Mr Zanuck ate in state, flanked by his producers. I didn't care about them. To me, the figures of glamor were the famous directors – gods!

There they were, ranged along the best wall, looking out over the enormous dining room, each at his reserved table with his favorite waitress, also reserved. The center tables were taken by the stars. They were surrounded by their favorites and sycophants: make-up men, hairdressers, stand-ins, agents, girl- or boyfriends. At other prominent tables sat the big men of the back lot, the cameramen. Each had his heads of departments, his gaffers and key grips and so on: a Homeric catalogue.

Only after several weeks did I notice and explore a sorry group at a remote table. Their isolation was so evident that it seemed planned. There was no mixing with this group, no table-hopping to their table. They seemed out of place. Their dress was tamer. Few had the fashionable suntan that a Beverly Hills success carries right to his grave. They laughed in a hysterical way, giddy or bitter. The writers . . .

Some of them were admitted hacks and some were unadmitted hacks. Some were top screenwriters. There would be an occasional Pulitzer Prize playwright or a famous novelist who had come out to do one screen assignment. Every last one of them seemed embarrassed to be there, and the embarrassment expressed itself in a bitter wit. They specialized in long sagas about the idiocy of the motion-picture business. There was a never-ending competition of appalling anecdotes. They made fun of everything and anybody – including themselves. A wealth of talent spent itself in mockery.

My education continued on the set of *Tree*. Since I was a total stranger to film, Lighton assigned me one of Hollywood's best cameramen, Leon Shamroy. I was to stage the scenes "as if they were happening in life"

Budd Schulberg, Father John Corriden (who inspired the character played by Karl Malden) and Elia Kazan, during the shooting of *On the Waterfront* (1954).

and Leon would decide how to photograph them. He would get onto film various angles that could subsequently be cut together to make an effective cinematic narration. Leon was a new experience to me. As I say, I'd come from Broadway where the writer was god and his lines were sacred by contract. Now I'm sure that Leon read the script, or most of it, before he started on the picture, but I know he didn't look at the day's scenes before coming to work each morning. This wasn't negligence; it was policy. There was a superstition that to look at the literary foliage would blur one's sense of the essential action. When I came on the set in the morning, he was usually there, a victim of sleep (too much or too little) and ready for the ministrations of the set porter. In those halcyon days, each set had its porter. In a daily ritual, Leon was presented with coffee – a Danish – the *Hollywood Daily Variety* – the *Hollywood Reporter*. While he read, I would earnestly rehearse the actors. In time, Leon would lower his *Reporter* and ask, "Well, what's the garbage for today?" The garbage was the dialogue. If he had a criticism, it was always the same one, "What do you need all those words for?" On his benign days, he didn't say garbage. He said, "the nonsense".

The writers were in a humiliating position. The motion-picture makers insisted on referring to themselves as an industry. An industry aspires to efficiency. They were supplying fifty-odd pictures per major studio per year to the market. They tried to supervise the manufacture of scripts by methods that worked splendidly in the automobile and heavy appliance industries. The system, with variations, went something like this.

An "original property" (a novel, a play, a "story idea") was bought outright. By this act, a studio acquired material and at the same time got rid of a potential troublemaker, the "original" author. (One of the tales that the writers told was about a studio head who bought a highly regarded bestseller. He strutted into his dining room and boasted, "I just bought a great story – but I think I can lick it!") The next step was an executive conference about the property and, usually, the casting of the stars. The "original property" was then turned over to a "construction man". His job was, precisely, to "lick the story". In other words, he was to bring the material into digestible shape and length, twist it to fit the stars and to eliminate unacceptable elements. These last included: elements banned by the Code; elements which might offend any section of the world audience; unentertaining elements such as unhappy endings or messages ("Leave them to Western Union!"). There was a word that governed what was cut out: the word "offbeat". This covered anything, really, that hadn't been done before, that hadn't been, as the marketing experts say, pre-tested. The "construction man", to put it simply, was supposed to lay down the outline of a hit. (For one reason, at this time, Middle Europeans were highly regarded for this job. Their knowledge of our language and country was slight but they were hell on structure and continuity.) Since the "construction man" was a specialist, the time came when his usefulness ended. Then, through his agent, he was invited to step out. A "dialogue man" was brought in. (The verb "to dialogue" was added to the Hollywood writers' glossary.) After the man who dialogued it, there frequently followed a "polish man". The script was getting close. (They hoped.) There was a good chance that an "additional dialogue man" would spend a few weeks on the job. His instructions might be very simple, as: "Put thirty laughs in it."

What was wrong with hiring a specialist in each field? It should have been efficient.

Trouble was, the final shooting script was so often preposterous. Characters went out of character. Plot threads got snarled. Climaxes made no sense because the preparation for them had got lost somewhere on the assembly line. If it was a "B" picture, they usually shot it anyway. But if it was a "big" picture, the producer, like

Lighton, would find himself late at night compiling a *last* final shooting script out of bits and pieces of all the previous versions. More often, it was the director who did this. Or sometimes, a brand-new writer was called in. The Screen Writers' Guild put in a lot of time ruling on which writers were entitled to what screen credit for a picture that none of them could altogether recognize.

2. It was all confusing, as I said, to a director fresh from the theatre. The theatre was Eugene O'Neill and Sidney Howard and Robert Sherwood and S. N. Behrman and Thornton Wilder and Clifford Odets and twenty others. The least, newest, greenest playwright shared the aura and the rights that the giants had earned. The rest of us – actors, directors and so on – knew that our function was to bring to life the plays they wrote.

But, I was told, pictures are different ... The difference comes from the power of the camera. Film is a pictorial medium. The strip of celluloid ought to tell the story with the sound track silent. There are crucial artistic choices that can't possibly be anticipated in a script. They have to be made hour by hour on the set and in the cutting room. A director stages plays; he *makes* pictures.

This was all true and I must confess that I took to it rather readily. Since I happened to be one, I was disinclined to quarrel with a line of reasoning which thrust power and pre-eminence upon the directors.

I was a good while longer learning certain other facts about picture-making. They are equally important. I learned them as I tripped up on inadequate scripts – including some that I vigorously helped to shape. I can state them with painful brevity.

There can't be a fine picture without a fine script.

There can't be a fine script without a first-class writer.

A first-class writer won't do first-class work unless he feels that the picture is *his*.

I doubt if the writer's place in pictures will – or should – ever be exactly the same as in the theatre, but I've been thinking lately about just what happened in the theatre. It's relevant and salutary.

Take 1900–1920. The theatre flourished all over the country. It had no competition. The box office boomed. The top original fare it had to offer was *The Girl of the Golden West*. Its bow to culture was fusty productions of Shakespeare. Either way, the plays were treated as showcases for stars. The business was in the hands of the managers and the actor-managers. The writers were nowhere. They were hacks who turned out new vehicles each season, to order. A playwright had about as little pride in his work, as little recognition for it, as little freedom, as a screenwriter in Hollywood in the palmy days. And his output was, to put it charitably, not any better ... Came the moving pictures. At first, they were written off as a fad. Then they began to compete for audiences and they grew until they threatened to take over. The theatre had to be better or go under. It got better. It got so spectacularly better so fast that in 1920–30 you wouldn't have recognized it. Perhaps it was an accident that Eugene O'Neill appeared at that moment but it was no accident that in that moment of strange competition, the theatre made room for him. Because it was disrupted and hard-pressed it made room for his experiments, his unheard-of subjects, his passion, his power. There was room for him to grow to his full stature. And there was freedom for the talents that came after his. For the first time, American writers turned to the theatre with anticipation and seriousness, knowing it could use the best they could give.

Lee J. Cobb in *On the Waterfront* (1954).

3. Well, now it's 1957 and television is the "industry". It's a giant – and a growing giant. It's fated to be much bigger than pictures ever were. Even now, it's overwhelming. We've all seen that. During the elections, during the World Series, during political crises, homes from coast to coast are tied to a few networks on the same cable, on the same timetable. Whether it's good or bad or both, one thing is certain: it's here.

Television is the subject of this second picture that Budd Schulberg and I have made together. It's also the force that's shaken up the whole picture business. It's our turn now. We in pictures have got to be better or go under.

When TV appeared, the motion-picture people put up a struggle. They didn't give up easily. First, they pretended that it wasn't there. Then they tried to combat it with every conceivable technical novelty. They tried big screens in all sorts of ratios of width to height. They tried the third dimension, with and without goggles. They tried multiple sound sources and bigger budgets. As I write, the novelty is long long long pictures. They tried just about

Patricia Neal and Andy Griffith in *A Face in the Crowd* (1956).

46

Andy Griffith in *A Face in the Crowd* (1956).

everything except the real novelty: three-dimensional material, new and better stories.

There are signs that they are being forced to that. It was hard to miss the meaning of the most recent Academy Awards. For 1953, *From Here to Eternity*; 1954, *On the Waterfront*; 1955, *Marty*. Of these, only the first came from a major studio. All three used ordinary old-fashioned screens. All three were shot in black and white. And different as they were, each of them was plainly, undeniably, "offbeat". People simply didn't care what size the screen was.

They went to see those pictures because they had life in them.

The writers rejoiced in a recognition that went beyond their awards, and notice that in each case the writer carried through from start to finish, working actively with the director. James Jones had written a hot novel out of his war experience. Daniel Taradash made the material his own, turned it into a fine screenplay and worked closely with Fred Zinnemann, the director. Budd Schulberg did an original screenplay out of long research and conviction and feeling, consulting with me often as he wrote, and standing by during much of the shooting. Paddy Chayefsky expanded his own television sketch into a picture and was consulted by Delbert Mann as it was being shot.

To get back to the picture-makers, they're in trouble. The box-office barometer dipped down, recovered, dropped again. Picture houses are closing, going dark. There is a rumor that one of the big studio lots is to be sold for a real-estate development. In such moments of confusion and panic, executive imaginations make unaccustomed flights. It has begun to occur to them that the writer – that eccentric, ornery, odd, unreliable, unreconstructed, independent fellow – is the only one who can give them real novelty.

The first sign that the old order was changing came in an odd but characteristic way: there was a certain loosening of the industry's self-imposed censorship Code. There were departures from the frantic and crippling rule that *You must please everybody; you can't offend anybody.* An older law was operating at the box office: if you try to please everybody, you don't please anybody.

At the same time, the unwritten taboos began to be relaxed. The superstition about "offbeat" material took a new turn. There seemed to be some mysterious plus in the "offbeat". Warily, story departments were instructed to look for subjects with this peculiar quality.

So now the writers – the fellows who used to sit in that clump in the farthest corner of the studio commissary – are being brought forward. A number of them have been moved "up" to non-writing jobs. They have been made producers and/or directors. Since it would seem obvious that writers are needed as writers, this may sound as inscrutably silly as other Hollywood behavior I've described – but it is at least a fumbling recognition that writers "have something" and that whatever it is, it's needed now. More reasonably, books and other stories that used to be thought unsuitable for pictures are being bought and tried. In a surprising number of cases, the "original author" is being asked to make his own screen version. Above all, writers are being invited, cajoled and very well paid to write original and serious pictures. This last is the big step and the big hope.

Another sign of change is the growing number of small independent units being financed by the big studios and operating with a freedom that was unimaginable ten years ago. The mood is, "Let them try..."

I'm one of the ones who's trying. I've formed my own company, Newtown Productions. I like being my own boss. I make my own pictures the way I want to make them. Also, I make my own mistakes. One of the things I've done, against all business advice, is to upset the traditional balance and make the writer more important than the stars. I don't think it's a mistake.

You see, I think we have a wonderful chance right now. The breakdown of the old standardized picture-making has made room for creative people. It is a boon to anyone who has something personal and strong to say. For art is nothing if it is not personal. It can't be homogenized. By its nature, it must disturb, stir up, enlighten and "offend".

I'd like to make one last point about the writers because it's important. To go back to the Academy Award winners, Dan Taradash and Budd Schulberg and Paddy Chayefsky, notice that they don't sneer at pictures. They don't think that screen writing is beneath them or that it's somehow an inferior form. The first time I met Budd, he had published three important and successful novels but he said to me, "God, I'd like to write a really good picture some day." I heard Paddy use almost the same words back in 1951 when he was a young TV writer. They have both done it. I think Budd has done it again.

I am writing these pages as a foreword to his screenplay for *A Face in the Crowd.* The very fact that it is published bespeaks

Andy Griffith in *A Face in
the Crowd* (1956).

With William Inge, who
wrote the screenplay for
Splendor in the Grass, on
the film set in 1961.

a new dignity. The way the picture was made tells a lot, too. I said earlier, we made it together. That tells the story.

After *Waterfront*, Budd and I decided to make another film, to be based on his short story, *Your Arkansas Traveler*. The impulse came partly from the story itself but even more from a series of conversations we had about – well, about everything. About TV – its power – hypnotic, potentially most dangerous and still, at times, brilliantly effective for good. We talked of how much more powerful Huey Long[1] would have been if he had had TV at his disposal. We talked about the famous Nixon broadcast, when the question of his financial backers turned somehow into a defence of his children's dog. We talked of the harm that Senator McCarthy did his own cause when he whispered direly to his young assistant in front of the cameras. We talked about the way public figures are now coached for their broadcasts and how the medium can make a performer or a politician overnight – or break a man that fast, too.

As we discussed the story, we began to watch programs much more than either of us had before. Every once in a while, something brilliant comes out of the box, like the reportage called *The First World War*, the Basilio–Saxton fight, Ed Murrow's interview with Colonel Nasser and his provocative visit to Clinton, Tenn., Yogi Berra leaping into Don Larsen's arms, Mary Martin and Ethel Merman. But TV, having won first place in the entertainment field, has the burdens of the victor. It has become the staple. It can't "offend". It's standard brand. And no matter how deeply you're drawn into what they're showing you, one of those fellows has got to come out and tell you with horrifying cheerfulness about soup or soap or cigarettes.

We took cognizance of the new synthetic folksiness that saturated certain programs and the excursions into political waters by these "I-don't-know-anything-but-I-know-what-I-think" guys. We wondered about the power of television to sell synthetic personalities as it sells the soup and the soap.

We went to Madison Avenue like explorers going into a strange country. We talked with performers and account executives and writers. We had interviews with big shots and lunch with medium-sized shots and drinks with little shots. We are indebted to all of them – not least for permission to sit in on a conference about the photographing of a ketchup bottle.

We listened and we read and we made notes and we compared notes and always we discussed what we had seen. Out of these conversations and the mutual desire to say something about this giant of our times came the shape of our picture.

Budd was the original source and, perhaps, the conscience. I was at his call and often at his side in the months he was writing it. He was at my side when my active work began. He was there during the casting and all the other preparation. We went to Piggott, Arkansas, together and decided that was the place to shoot the country scenes. He came there on location and, also, to Memphis. He has been on the set every day in New York and made essential contributions. I never worked more closely with an author in the theatre.

And as for the lunch hour, we ate together.

With John Steinbeck, who wrote the script for *Viva Zapata!* (1951).

¹The conservative Governor of Louisiana, who inspired Robert Penn Warren's novel, *All the King's Men.*

MY CHIEF ARTISTIC COLLABORATORS: DIRECTORS OF PHOTOGRAPHY

In my film work the collaborators I valued most were the cameramen. Since I came from the theatre where the spoken word is so essential, I had to be jolted into realizing that the eye not the ear was the most important sense, that a film's story is told by a sequence of images and that, very often, the less dialogue there is the better, that if a film could be told entirely by pictures, that would be best of all. I was forced to learn this lesson straight off on my very first film. There I experienced the essen-tial shock. My cameraman was a grumpy fellow whom I came to love. His name was Leon Shamroy and his nickname with the crew was "Grumble-gut". He immediately set back the cocky young fellow from the New York stage (me) by arriving for work every morning with only the vaguest acquaintance with the text for that day's work. "What's the garbage for today?" he'd ask in his rasping voice. "Why the hell didn't you read the script?" I'd come back. "I'd rather watch a rehearsal," he'd say.

With director of photography Harry Stradling, on the set of *The Sea of Grass* (1946).

"That will tell the story." I soon came to see that his point of view, while extreme, was essentially the correct one, that I should photograph behavior, not "talking heads". With this realization in mind, I began to study the work of the great directors. I marvelled at how long Jack Ford would hold a long shot and how much it would tell, what imagination and daring he had. Watching his work and that of other directors I admired, I realized that all I'd been doing was photographing action of a kind that predominates on a stage, staying mostly in medium shots with a close-up now and then to "punch home" a point or make an emphasis. In every difficulty, I'd rely on the spoken word rather than a revealing image.

So the cameramen became my best friends in California. I thought most producers ignorant, inept bluffers. I thought the same of many directors, noting how heavily they relied on their cameramen to tell them where to put the camera down and what to do with it. Also, despite my reputation as an "actor's director", I did not find most actors stimulating artistic collaborators. There were exceptions, but if I were to choose a generalization that would be true for me, I'd say that my allegiance shifted from words to the camera and to the cameramen. I felt that, even more than the director, they were "on the spot"; they had to produce a piece of film every day that would be used in the final picture. They had to make good, as we say, and no excuses would be accepted.

I also responded with affection and enthusiasm to their vitality and their pleasure – ability. They would experience what I would, the challenge and the fun of film-making not budget-making. They were handymen and I admired that too, would work in any weather, hot, cold, rain, snow, or under a burning sun. They were also enthusiastic improvisers and would get through any and all difficult times, one way or another. Nothing could set them back. When I was "stuck" they would suggest solutions, and I came to rely on them more

and more and to confide in them increasingly. Only to them would I confide my ultimate intentions and dreams with relation to a film; to them and not to anyone else. I noticed that often when a scenic problem would worry me, it would exhilarate a cameraman.

All the cameramen I worked with were "great", a word that's been cheapened by overuse by show-business media people. If I were asked to choose one cameraman above the others, I'd refuse. But if a pistol was put to my head, I'd say Boris Kaufman. I remember that time after time I'd arrive on the location of the film-making with a very definite idea of how to approach that day's work and specifically how to shoot the basic first shot, that is from where. I'd tell Boris what my conviction was, if I had a conviction. He'd walk with me to the position I was suggesting to launch the point of

Elia Kazan (*left*) beside his director of photography Boris Kaufman, on the set of *Baby Doll* (1956).

view for the day's work, he'd examine what I was offering him, listen to me, then say with crushing modesty, "Suppose we study it from another place – just to see." Then add, "For the challenge of it." Then not at all bending to the producer's constant and inevitable prodding ("Get the first shot early in the can. If you do that, you'll have a good day's work") I'd walk slowly to the position he suggested and in a slow, that is a civilized rhythm, we'd study the scene as it would be photographed from that point of view. Very often the pictorial approach he was suggesting was better than mine. But above all he taught me to stop and consider, to study all possibilities before plunging into an irrevocable decision. For Boris there was always the grace of patience and comradely consideration, weighing one attack against every other. He was a true artist and I remember him with love.

The only cameraman I did not like personally was Haskell Wexler. But he was an excellent cameraman. He turned out to be further left politically than I believed when I engaged him and I felt a certain resentment of me from him, of a kind with which I'd become familiar. We were in Turkey so I could not replace him easily, but I didn't replace him for another reason: I saw that he would help me with my work. I respected him as a craftsman but I disliked him as a man, thought him typical of many left-wing intellectuals. I also didn't like the crew he'd assembled. A cameraman's crew tells who he is. Perhaps too I couldn't take his insulting manner with me: a kind of left-wing snobbery I believed it to be. He said to me one day, "You know you don't have a good eye." I resented that remark for years, but I resented even more what he said when the film was done: "I think I can see what you were getting at now," this after weeks and weeks together. About twenty years after *America America* was released, he wrote me that he'd seen the film at a film festival and thought it a "great, enduring movie". He thanked me for giving him the chance to be part of it. By then I didn't care. It was too late.

With his director of photography Robert Surtees (*in glasses, standing*) on the set of *The Arrangement* (1969).

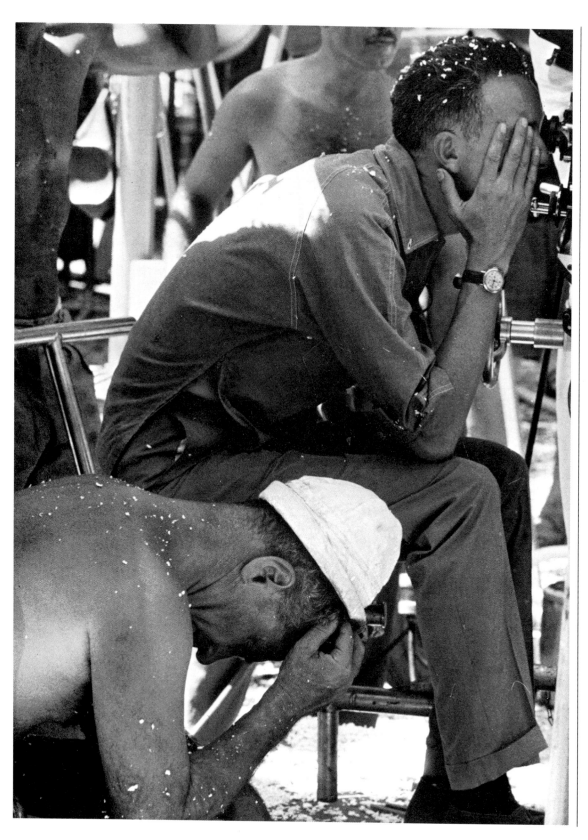

With director of
photography Haskell
Wexler (*behind*) on the set
of *America America*
(1964).

With director of photography Haskell Wexler (*left*) on the set of *America America* (1964).

The thing I like most about cameramen is a human quality: they actually enjoy the job of making a film, the work itself. Producers worry and wait for the end of shooting, sometimes to see if they can take the editing process away from the director. So they reveal themselves to be the director's enemy. Actors worry about their performance, whether it's a step forward or backward in the agent-market. Screenwriters sweat with fear, often believing that a director is lousing up their script. But the cameramen I've known and their crews come to work with joy; they come to "play". They're the men for me. Where a producer resents rain and smoke and snow and the movement of the clouds over the sun because they delay production, cameramen love these events of nature. Extreme cold or a burning sun make an actor look less like an actor and more like an ordinary human being.

The cameraman I had the most fun with was Harry Stradling; he was a fearless person and could do anything and do it fast, give you two close-ups at the end of the afternoon as the light was going in fifteen minutes. Nothing fazed him and he could move the lights himself if he had to. He also always had a congenial bottle handy and at the end of the day's work we'd enjoy drinking and laughing together. The niftiest and gutsiest of them all was Joe MacDonald and perhaps the most beloved by his crew. He brightened each day we worked. The most dignified of them all and a man I liked very much was Ellsworth Fredericks. He always wore a city hat even when we worked in the deep countryside of the state of Tennessee.

"Be bold!" I used to cry out to them all; that was all the encouragement they needed to take a new tack, a fresh approach and to respond with the unexpected. I never said, "Be careful."

Everything I liked best in my favorite cameramen – their adventurousness, their fearlessness, their love of the work, their professional energy and expertise – was combined in the character of my favorite costume designer, Anna Hill Johnstone. Nothing, no problem, no emergency ever daunted her. Anywhere I took her, she'd go costume the people in the bottom of society as well as those in the middle class. Of all the people I've ever worked with, she was the one I most trusted.

Costume sketches for *America America* by Anna Hill Johnstone (1) Stathis Giallelis, (2) Linda Marsh, (3) Gregory Rozakis, (4) Katharine Balfour, (5) John Marley, (6) Estelle Hemsley, (7) Robert Harris.

The same dauntless energy characterized Gene Callahan, my art director, which means scene designer. I particularly remember how he bullied a recalcitrant and indifferent crew in the Near East to do work for me. When I think of him I feel the greatest gratitude.

AMERICA AMERICA
ARTISTS GREGORY ROZAKIS
AS HOHANNESS
SCENE NO. 1 SCENE 396
EXT
KAZAN JOHNSTONE

Sophia-Kath Balser
Carpet Co-
aa Palace   Earring

AMERICA AMERICA
ARTISTS ESTELLE HEMSLEY
AS GRANDMOTHER
CHANGE SCENE 133-142
EXT:
KAZAN JOHNSTONE

Robert HARRIS
ARATOON
Ship

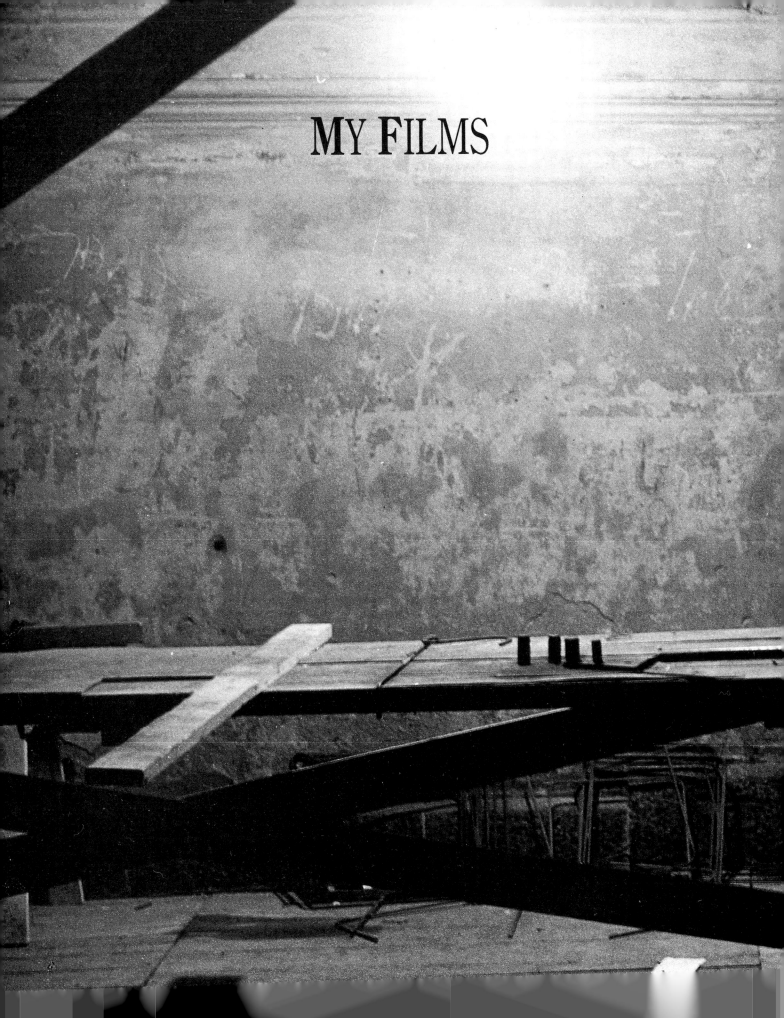

MY FILMS

A TREE GROWS IN BROOKLYN

These film notes were written specially for this book.

This was my first big studio film. I'd fooled around before with a camera and a friend – but this was "serious". Professionally a great deal depends on the impression a first picture makes, not only on the money but on yourself. You find you're either "taking to it" or you're not. I did. I also had luck. I found a child actress, Peggy Ann Garner, who was as good as anything I could have hoped for. In the middle of our elaborate and carefully built Hollywood set was this one absolutely true thing: Peggy's face. Oh, I had another piece of luck; I stumbled on Jimmy Dunn to play her father with a drinking problem. I think Jimmy had. At any rate, he made me believe he had, which is the point. And another piece of luck: a kind and sensitive old line producer who spoke to me about feeling, emotion, conviction – not about effects and jokes. They all made this first film a joy. It was a success and I was established.

Peggy Ann Garner and Ted Donaldson in *A Tree Grows in Brooklyn* (1944).

Preceding page: Elia Kazan on a visit to Sweden (1961).
Opposite: Joan Blondell in *A Tree Grows in Brooklyn* (1944).

THE SEA OF GRASS

So now I had some power to choose what I'd do next and I immediately chose the wrong thing. I was naïve, which made it worse. I thought I was going to be doing a great epic of the great open country – like *Cimarron* or *Red River*. Instead I found myself a prisoner on the great closed MGM lot. I was always within walking distance of the Commissary and the barber's shop. My problem was simple: I had two great stars and a couple more near great. Spencer Tracy, who played the lord of the house, never won the friendship of his horse, not even the tolerance. Katharine Hepburn came trotting out every morning in another designer period dress. They were both agreeable and entertaining people to be with and I enjoyed our conversations but I didn't enjoy the film-making. It received what it deserved – a very bad reception.

Robert Walker in *The Sea of Grass* (1946).

Left: Katharine Hepburn and Spencer Tracy in *The Sea of Grass* (1946).

Right: Melvyn Douglas and Katharine Hepburn in *The Sea of Grass* (1946).

BOOMERANG

I decided on a drastic course: to make a film with no studio settings and no stars. Well, we had sort of a star but he fitted right in. As for the rest, they were my "gang of actors" from the Actors' Studio. They looked like the people of the city of Stamford, Connecticut who were my "extras". I shot the scenes where they actually took place, on the streets, in the city jail, in the county court room and so on. It was a joy – this way to make pictures – and I recognized this was my natural milieu – not the big studio. Furthermore the picture was a success.

Left: Dana Andrews in *Boomerang* (1946).

Below: Boomerang (1946).

Left: Lee J. Cobb, Karl Malden and Dana Andrews in *Boomerang* (1946).

Karl Malden and Arthur Kennedy in *Boomerang* (1946).

GENTLEMAN'S AGREEMENT

This was a cause movie, anti-anti-semi-tism. It was to be Fox's and Zanuck's picture of the year and there was a fine man, Moss Hart, writing our script. Being what I was, a *liberal*, I embraced the project eagerly. I had a top-flight cast and I can't remember any of their performances. It was shot with the best set designer and the best costume designer and the best cameraman and everything was so expert, which is to say smoothly conventional that there is not a single scene from the film that I can recall. But Zanuck knew his business; he put together everything, the people and the technicians, so expertly that the film won the Academy Award. I did too. But I do not consider my direction anything more than conventional and expert. There wasn't a surprise in the film. Acclaimed in 1946, it is rarely seen now. I came out of it famous in the industry.

John Garfield and Celeste Holm in *Gentleman's Agreement* (1947).

68

Gregory Peck, Dorothy McGuire, Celeste Holm and John Garfield in *Gentleman's Agreement* (1947).

PINKY

Don't blame this one on me. I don't. I didn't help prepare the script. I didn't have the idea of casting a most genteel, middle-class white girl as a light-skin black. I didn't agree again to shoot real locations on studio sets. That was all Jack Ford's idea. After ten days of work he got sick and had to withdraw and Zanuck asked me to do him a favor and take over. I hadn't yet learned how to say no. Again outdoor scenes inside a sound stage – even scenes of violence on a bridge. I was handsomely paid for any little work and I bought a place in the Connecticut countryside. It was a painless experience – until I saw the result – which was also painless, the pain that true drama should cause. I was becoming something I didn't want to be, an "actor's director". An expert at moving anybody around for a camera. What I wanted to be was a film-maker.

Ethel Waters and Jeanne Crain in *Pinky* (1949).

Ethel Barrymore and
Ethel Waters in *Pinky*
(1949).

Jeanne Crain, Nina
McKinney and Frederick
O'Neal in *Pinky* (1949).

PANIC
IN THE STREETS

I took a drastic step – I made up my mind to make a film in the style of one of my heroes, Jack Ford, a film that could be understood using only the eyes of a deaf person. And to shoot it in the style I had found to be my own – on location, without a set, everything real, true, ordinary, totally convincing. And no Hollywood stars. I would take my camera places a movie camera had never been before. I did. The whole city of New Orleans was my set and I used a lot of it. Again I used actors who were known only to New York theatre people. I'd found my true course.

Emile Meyer, Paul
Douglas and Richard
Widmark in *Panic in the
Streets* (1950).

Jack Palance in *Panic in
the Streets* (1950).
Opposite: Zero Mostel in
Panic in the Streets (1950).

A STREETCAR NAMED DESIRE

Again friendship threw me off my course. I'd done the play and had become the artistic partner of Tennessee Williams. When he asked me to make the film, I refused. When he asked me the second time, I couldn't refuse. I said I'd do it if I could with my New York cast. Agreed except for Blanche. Warner Brothers insisted on a big star in that part. Again I hesitated – too late. They'd agreed to all my other demands. Can you believe they would have preferred someone not Brando? Or Jimmy Cagney to Karl Malden as Mitch? No. I could have it all my way except for Vivien Leigh. She had an advantage, they told me; she'd played it on stage too – in London. This was the opposite of an advantage. It took me three weeks to get her to do the part *my* way, not Larry Olivier's way. But then she began to yield and we began to be friends. I began to admire her. She had more grit than talent but determination and courage she had to an extraordinary degree. At the end, I admired her a great deal. Contrary to rumor, she got along with my New York gang very well, particularly Marlon; she admired him greatly.

Kim Hunter and Marlon Brando in *A Streetcar Named Desire* (1950).

Marlon Brando and Vivien
Leigh in *A Streetcar
Named Desire* (1950).

A ZAPATA!

Why did I make *Viva Zapata!*? The reason was political and of the most naïve kind: hero worship. Zapata fulfilled his revolutionary goals, then when he found that this sudden power was corrupting him, turned his back and walked away. That year of my life, 1951–2, was when I was turning against the ideals of Communism and its program of social struggle. To our surprise, John Steinbeck and I found we had the same convictions, the same enthusiasms and finally the same question: how could this man, who'd led his country people through a long and bloody civil war, have won his goals, then rejected the power he'd gained on a mysterious impulse of personal principle? That extraordinary event needed understanding – or at least contemplation. John and I had found a hero at a time when we had no other. Here was a symbolic act to hold up for admiration.

Marlon Brando in *Viva Zapata!* (1951).

I thought that with *Panic* and *Boomerang* I'd learned the value and the technique of shooting out in the open country. I had not. I was still a stage-bound director. This film was my liberation. How? Because I found myself incapable, and had to ask for help and guidance. Well, it was a big joke, I'd never have a bigger, to photograph a whole circus, albeit a small one, crossing a bridge between Communist Czechoslovakia and free Austria. I learned by shortcomings, I learned the uses of fortitude, energy, courage, daring. I became, with this film, the man who made *On the Waterfront* – and didn't need help on that.

MAN ON A TIGHTROPE

Fredric March in *Man on a Tightrope* (1952).

Opposite: Fredric March and Terry Moore in *Man on a Tightrope* (1952). *Left:* Gloria Grahame in *Man on a Tightrope* (1952).

79

ON THE WATERFRONT

Karl Malden in *On the Waterfront* (1954).

Exactly. And on the streets, in the alleys, on the rooftops, they all came together here, my experiences. This project was turned down by every "big" studio in California and twice by Columbia, the company which finally financed it. In it Mr Brando gives the best male performance I've ever seen by an actor. Period. I do not add "in the country". It is a perfect performance. And everything we learned in the Group Theatre bore fruit here. The other actors are on the same level, superb. Lee Cobb was never better. Rod Steiger gave a memorable performance. Eva Marie Saint, a revelation. Karl Malden, in the most diffi-

cult part, did himself, and me, full credit. This is the first film I ventured that I am proud of without qualification. I'd made up my mind to bring fine writers to films. I did. Here is Budd Schulberg, who wrote a film classic. For a reason I don't understand, this film is less admired in France and England than it should be. Some critics even concede it "Fascist". Despite any and all criticism, it is my most successful and my best-known film in this country. But it is not my favorite.

Marlon Brando and Eva
Marie Saint in *On the
Waterfront* (1954).

Karl Malden, Marlon
Brando and Eva Marie
Saint in *On the Waterfront*
(1954).

EAST OF EDEN

With the success of *Waterfront*, I could do any film I wanted to do and I chose *East of Eden*. I also had, at last, the recognition film directors who work in the industry want most: final cut, which means that my film goes into theatres the way I want it to. This privilege, hard-earned, lasts as long as one's films make money. I also had the right to cast my films as I wished and, in my case, that was without Hollywood stars, with what people had begun to call my New York stock company. I did, however, find a new actor for the leading role, a young man who had some mystery in his personality which was to make him even more popular than Marlon Brando. James Dean represented something to the young people of this country which was emblematic of their struggle with authority and particularly

their parents. This was the most auto-biographical film I'd made until this time; the character Dean played represented a side of me that I believed my own father had misunderstood and not appreciated. I am often asked what it was like directing Dean and Brando. The answer, once and for all, is that it was simple. The actors who are difficult to direct are those who have no talent or are unsuited to the roles they played. I can't say that I, as a five-time parent, truly appreciated Jimmy's symbolic meaning to the youth here; in fact I regretted it. I had one great blessing on the film and her name was Julie Harris. Playing opposite Dean she did a great deal to get him through his first film.

James Dean, Julie Harris and Richard Davalos in *East of Eden* (1954).

Opposite: Jo Van Fleet, James Dean and Richard Davalos in *East of Eden* (1954).

BABY DOLL

Carroll Baker and Karl
Malden in *Baby Doll*
(1956).

I'd talked to Tennessee Williams about this material ever since *Streetcar* and finally having the power that only commercial success brings in this country, I was able to make it. This time I used only Actors' Studio people plus the natives of that region of Mississippi where I shot the film. This is a film of mine that people have taken too seriously: it is a "black comedy" and was so intended, not a criticism of the soul of the South. I like the South and the people there very much and I believe my affection shows in the scenes. Again I had good luck; I found an excellent young actress at the Actors' Studio who fulfilled the role, and along with Eli Wallach and Karl Malden made a cast unique for a big studio American picture. The film drew undeserved notoriety because of the foolish actions of Cardinal Spellman, a dunce, who caused the film to be condemned by the Roman Catholic church.

Carroll Baker in *Baby Doll*
(1956).
Opposite: Carroll Baker
and Eli Wallach in *Baby
Doll* (1956).

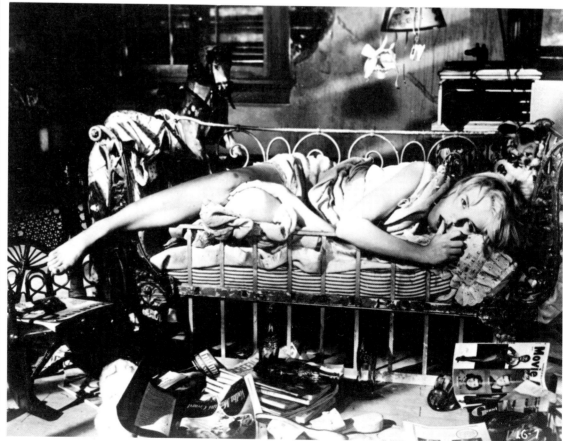

A FACE IN THE CROWD

Andy Griffith in *A Face in the Crowd* (1956).

With *East of Eden* another great success my fame was reaching mythic proportions. Time, of course, would correct this. Again I was privileged – or was it Warner Brothers, who were privileged – to make the picture I chose and make it my own way. Both Budd Schulberg (who had written *Waterfront*) and I, looking just a little ahead, were concerned about the power of TV to influence and sway people. We saw it could alter the way political campaigns were run in this country and bring on for high office men who were performers more than statesmen. Of course our fore-sight turned out to be true. Again I cast this film altogether with my New York "stock company", plus a leading man out of Nashville country music, Andy Griffith. And once again I had the good fortune to find two wonderful young actresses to support him. I believe the film turned out well. And it endured. I myself particularly enjoy this film and it makes me laugh more than any other film I made. But it is not my favorite – only one of them.

Patricia Neal in *A Face in the Crowd* (1956).

WILD RIVER

This is one of my favorite films and of them all the most neglected. It draws on my memories of the New Deal and the Tennessee Valley Authority which built great dams in the mid-south of our country to bring inexpensive electrical power to the people of that region. This meant that certain large, low levels would be flooded and our story takes place in one of those areas. An old woman refuses to give up her home to "progress" and the story is of how she is finally brought to leave. In the role of this woman and her daughter are two magnificent actresses from the Actors' Studio, Jo Van Fleet and Lee Remick. All through this period I had great good fortune with my actresses. However, this film, like some others that I particularly favor, was a box-office disaster. It is never shown in the United States and except for certain discerning and sensitive critics in Europe might have been completely forgotten. I'm particularly proud of this neglected work.

Montgomery Clift and Lee Remick in *Wild River* (1960).

Lee Remick in *Wild River* (1960).

Opposite: Jo Van Fleet in *Wild River* (1960).

John McGovern and
Natalie Wood in *Splendor
in the Grass* (1960).

Warren Beatty and
Barbara Loden in *Splendor
in the Grass* (1960).

SPLENDOR
IN THE GRASS

Warren Beatty and Natalie Wood in *Splendor in the Grass* (1961).

Splendor in the Grass is very much like a certain kind of European film. But then, after all the years and despite all my participation in American life, I am still part European. The film has the quality of its author, Bill Inge, a man I greatly esteemed. It starts with an engaging and deceptive innocence, seems bland and conventional, then begins to go deeper and finally to hurt. A soap opera turns tragic. The last reel may be my favorite last reel of any in the films I've made. Not many of the films I particularly like have been commercial successes, but this one was – modestly. One reason is the acting – my stock company again, all or mostly all from the Actors' Studio, with the addition of Natalie Wood and an absolute newcomer named Warren Beatty. At this time this star-to-be was a rather awkward, gawky boy just right for a High School senior trying to get out from under the influence of his father. But the main reason for the film's worth is the subtle and unobtrusive story-telling of Inge and his humanity. I believe this is the preferred film of many French critics, Bertrand Tavernier (now a film director) for instance, but although it is a film I like very much, it is not my favorite film.

AMERICA AMERICA

This is my favorite among the films I've made, not because it's my best film but because I wrote it and made it and because it's about the subject I spent years contemplating: how my family came to America. The incidents in the film are all true if somewhat dramatized and were told me by my grandmother and my mother. I started shooting it in Turkey, which was my wish, but the authorities there, suspicious of my intentions and point of view, insisted on having their censor on the set. They also had a member of their secret police observing this censor to make sure he did his job well. This kind of pressure became intolerable and we moved the production to Greece, which is a free country, and made it there happily. The picture touches memories of many people, not only Anatolian Greeks – which is what I am – but people of every other nationality who managed to make the journey to the States. It also represents my statement of gratitude to this country. With all that, it is a simple story of family love and of a very small man's adventures in a rough world. This film too was a financial disaster and after it my privileges as a film-maker – my own cast and story, final cut and so on – were no longer available to me.

Lou Antonio and Stathis Giallelis in *America America* (1964).

Stathis Giallelis in *America America* (1964).

THE ARRANGEMENT

Now certain events – the death of my wife after thirty-one years of marriage – changed my life. The financial failure of so many of my favorite films, *America America, Wild River, Viva Zapata!, A Face in the Crowd, Baby Doll*, also affected me in a most practical sense. It became impossible for me now to make the films I wanted or the way I wanted. So I turned to writing; I wrote a novel, *The Arrangement*, which was an enormous – and surprising – success. It was so successful that for a brief spell I was again sought after by the industry. I was offered a large sum of money to make a film of the book and, having the expenses that many men with a large family have, I decided to do it. The cast is not the one I wanted, but I'd made the mistake of taking some money in advance and had to make the picture, in the end, with the best cast available to me. They were all good actors but not quite what I originally had in mind, and the film was better than the critics believed it to be but again not quite conforming to my original vision. Although the book continued to sell – and still does – this film was another financial disaster. I recommend it to you.

Right: Faye Dunaway in *The Arrangement* (1969).
Below: Deborah Kerr and Kirk Douglas in *The Arrangement* (1969).

Below right: Faye Dunaway and Kirk Douglas in *The Arrangement* (1969).

Deborah Kerr and Harold
Gould in *The Arrangement*
(1969).

Kirk Douglas and Deborah
Kerr in *The Arrangement*
(1969).

So I went on writing novels. They were all published immediately and the point of view, material and treatment were entirely my own. I thought the amount of money spent on *The Arrangement*, three times more than on any other film I'd ever made, was absurd and I wished to return to the purity of poverty, in other words to show that film-making was basically a single and most human endeavor and did not require an enormous structure of machinery and equipment and the overhead costs which that brings with it. My son, Chris, and I were discussing the effect of the war in Vietnam on the United States' civilian population and a news item in a newspaper struck us. Chris wrote an excellent shooting script and we found five totally unknown actors and made it on the piece of land in Connecticut where we both live. Our film pre-dates all other films with this theme. It also seems to have offended many critics and members of the audience in the United States, I don't understand why. It was a financial disaster, but I heartily recommend it to you.

Patrick McVey and Patricia Joyce in *The Visitors* (1971).

Patrick McVey and Steve Railsback in *The Visitors* (1971).

James Woods in *The Visitors* (1971).

97

THE LAST TYCOON

Jack Nicholson in *The Last Tycoon* (1976).

The reasons why I did this film are mysterious and personal. I had nothing to do with preparing the script and, in one very central respect, I was dissatisfied with it. But the film has a remarkable performance by Robert De Niro and it's worth seeing. There are other good enough performances, but that of De Niro is surprising. For reasons that are irrelevant to my own way of film-making, I made it in a big California studio, something I'd promised myself not to do. My personal life was in a turmoil – my mother died in my house in Beverly Hills as we shot it and I was breaking up with my second wife – but again, despite the fact it was a financial disaster, I recommend the film to you. It has a mostly very interesting script by Harold Pinter, whom I admire, and when I made the film I believed that the last shot was my final bow on leaving the stage.

Ray Milland and Robert Mitchum in *The Last Tycoon* (1976).

Opposite: Robert De Niro and Ingrid Boulting in *The Last Tycoon* (1976).

98

5301-22

A LETTER ON *VIVA ZAPATA!*

Letter to the
Saturday Review
(May 24th, 1952).

SIR: There has been an eloquent criticism of *Viva Zapata!* in the *Saturday Review* (February 9th) and also an eloquent defense by Laura Z. Hobson (March 1st). That is as much discussion as any motion picture deserves and I do not want to add to it. However, your readers may be interested to hear how the political tensions of the present bore down on us – John Steinbeck and Darryl Zanuck and me – as we thought about and shaped a historical picture. These pressures, though nerve-racking, forced us to clear our own perspectives and in this sense were useful. They also brought to me a realization of the relationship between abstract politics and personal character which I had not formulated before.

It is human character, above all, which concerns a director, writer, producer, and it was the character of Zapata which intrigued us all. He was not a man of words and what he was had to be read in what he did. Part of our interest in the beginning lay in a certain mystery about what kind of man he really was.

It was not the first and simpler part of his story which suggested an almost unique man. He had risen from nothing, illiterate, uneloquent, to overthrow the forty-year dictatorship of the "Permanent President" Diaz. He had challenged a disorganized 1910-version of the police state. He had formed and led an army. He led it with bravery, tenacity, and an astounding, untutored military skill.

Yet there were other leaders, some also brave and tenacious and effective in battle. What fascinated us about Zapata was one nakedly dramatic act. In the moment of victory, he turned his back on power. In that moment, in the capital with his ragged troops, Zapata could have made himself president, dictator, caudillo. Instead, abruptly and without explanation, he rode back to his village. There he saw to it that the people got back their farms, which had been taken from them, and there, as he must have known would happen, he was hunted down by men who had no scruple about taking power or using it to stamp out opposition.

We felt this act of renunciation was the high point of our story and the key to Zapata himself. If we could not explain it, we did not know our man. Yet no written account gave an acceptable explanation.

We went to Morelos, Steinbeck and I, and saw the dry austere grandeur of the mountains, the poverty of the fields, the poverty and pride and almost Biblical dignity of the

Anthony Quinn and Marlon Brando in *Viva Zapata!* (1951).

people. And here we walked into an attack from – call it left field.

We knew that the Communists in Mexico try to capitalize on the people's reverence for Zapata by working his figure into their propaganda – much as Communists here quote Lincoln to their purpose. We had ignored this and gone about our business, for we knew that Communists anywhere always will try to appropriate anything to which people give allegiance – peace, pros-

[1]Communist Party newspaper.

Opposite: Marlon Brando and Jean Peters in *Viva Zapata!* (1951).

perity, land reform, brotherhood, democracy, equality, liberty, nationalism, internationalism, free speech, or whatever. We can hardly give over these things to their claim.

So it was that, with our minds on the picture business and not on politics, we approached two men who are prominent in the Mexican film industry. We had some idea that we might want them to work with us and in any case, humbly, as foreigners writing about their national hero, we asked their opinion of our preliminary script.

They came back with an attack that left us reeling. The script was impossible! We listened. We discovered they were attacking us for including things which we knew to be historically true: that Zapata had a measure of Spanish blood and was proud of it, the very proper Spanish-colonial style of his courtship and marriage, his vanity in the matter of dress and uniform, his abandoning of the white cotton peon costume when he could afford to, his indecision about taking up arms. But above all, they attacked with sarcastic fury our emphasis on his refusal to take power.

We digested all this on the terrace of the Hotel Marik in Cuernavaca. Four feet away, on the other side of a low wall, the Indians went by in the street. Over the houses the mountains loomed and the air was soft. John said, "I smell the Party line."

I smelled it too. Nearly two years later our guess was confirmed by a rabid attack on the picture in the *Daily Worker*[1] which parallels everything the two Mexicans argued, and which all but implies that John invented Zapata's renunciation of power.

No Communist, no totalitarian, ever refused power.

By showing that Zapata did this, we spoiled a poster figure that the Communists have been at some pains to create. As we figured this out, we saw our man more

Marlon Brando in *Viva Zapata!* (1951).

clearly, and were readier for the attack from the opposite political pole.

It had to come. Whenever the Communists stake a claim to any concept or person that people value, the over-anxious Right plays into their hands with exasperating regularity. If they would treat the Communist claim to peace, to free speech – and to men like Zapata – with the same good sense and laughter that greets the Communist claim to the invention of the bicycle, it would make life easier for those of us who really value those things.

In any case, we were told by an organization long on vigilance but short on history that Zapata was a rebel, so he must have been a Communist. There was, of course, no such thing as a Communist Party at the time and place where Zapata fought. (The *Daily Worker* regrets it.) But there is such a thing as a Communist mentality. We created a figure of this complexion in Fernando, whom the audience identify as "the man with the typewriter". He typifies the men who use the just grievances of the people for their own ends, who shift and twist their course, betray any friend or principle or promise to get power and keep it.

Thinking thus – not of politics but of human behavior – we saw Zapata clearly. In his moment of decision, this taciturn, untaught leader must have felt, freshly and deeply, the impact of the ancient law: power cor-

Marlon Brando and Joseph Wiseman in *Viva Zapata!* (1951).

Lou Gilbert, Margo and
Harold Gordon in *Viva
Zapata!* (1951).

rupts. And so he refused power.

The man who refused power was not only
no Communist, he was that opposite phe-
nomenon: a man of individual conscience.

For confirmation, we had seen the people
whom he led. No weakling, no trickster, no
totalitarian, leaves behind him a strong
people, but the men of Morelos are
respected today as the proudest and most
independent in all Mexico. Their bearing is
proof of the kind of man who led them out of
bondage and did not betray them. I think it
is also witness to the relationship of two
things not usually coupled: politics and
human dignity.

YOU HAVE TO START A FILM TWICE

It has always seemed to me that a director has to commit himself twice to the making of a picture. The first time, he makes up his mind. The important time is the second, when he accepts his material with full emotional belief.

Take *Man on a Tightrope*. A circus breaks through the Iron Curtain ... In one sentence, that's a good story. The first time I heard it, I liked it. I signed to make it.

As soon as I signed, I felt uneasy. I didn't quite believe the story. The fact that a small circus, the Brumbach Circus, had actually escaped into West Germany was no help. It registered logically, but I had no kinship with the experience. The Iron Curtain was not real to me. It was a figure of speech. An abstraction. The armed boundary, the terror behind it, were things I had read about. I had not seen or felt them.

I flew to Bavaria to look for locations, to look for conviction. I found both. It is hard to summarize weeks of experiences. I will try to suggest them.

There was the border itself. I saw four points where roads crossed it, one where the Freedom Train had broken through a year earlier. On our side, there would be a little customs house converted to a guard house, a ditch, a roadblock. On their side, long low troop barracks, watch-towers under construction, barbed wire, electrified wire, bared fields, a silent town evacuated to create a cleared zone. Seeing the empty town through borrowed field glasses, seeing the insulators on the wire, I began to feel what this border means. The Communist precautions are not against military attack, they are to prevent the escape of their own people. The guard explains that each month the devices are strengthened. Now the fields are mined.

He sometimes hears the mines go off at night, "Rabbits, mostly. You can't tell."

Then there was the story, told by a US State Department man, of a fellow who was smuggled over last summer under the hood of a car. He lay across the engine. He arrived badly burned.

Everywhere there was this taking for granted of the terror on the other side, of the risks people would take to escape it.

There was Camp Valka outside Nuremberg, almost in sight of Hitler's grandiose unfinished stadium. Here many escapees are housed and here the International Rescue Committee tries, with woefully inadequate funds, to provide welcome and assistance. (The Bavarians have no extra food, housing, jobs, to share with the arrivals.) A far better record than average, for instance, is that of eleven uranium miners who escaped: situations have been found for nine of them. The other two were still at the camp. Both have TB. They seemed quick-minded fine men, humorous in their talk, but the long idle months were taking a toll. Their horizon of hope was narrow indeed.

There were the performers and backstage men and families of the Brumbach Circus who signed to work in the picture. In no sense political people, they are simply among those who found life intolerable under Communist control and made their dangerous escape when the future promised to be worse.

Then there was the episode of the cameraman. This picture would be the first by a major American studio to employ an all-German crew. We were assured that it would be a great honor for the cameraman selected. We ran a lot of pictures and

picked our man and interviewed him. He seemed less honored than worried. He took the assignment with plain hesitation. The week before we were to start shooting, he quit.

He explained that he owned a house in East Berlin. It was currently appropriated for government use but he still held title. If he made this picture, it would be confiscated for good. But besides this between jobs he lived in West Berlin. If he made this picture, he was fearful of what might happen when he passed through the Russian Zone on his way home. He had been going over

and over this in his mind for a week and more and he was truly nervous. His wife had come down from Berlin to urge him to make the picture if he really wanted, but he was afraid. He begged us to understand.

His resignation was rumored on the picture lot. Another cameraman, Georg Krause, was suggested to replace him. Krause told us about his background the hesitant way a man does when he applies for a job. Then he burst out, "I also own a house in East Berlin. I don't care if I lose it. We lived there for one year after the war, I and my wife and two girls, with an officer of the

Gloria Grahame in *Man on a Tightrope* (1952).

107

Adolphe Menjou in *Man on a Tightrope* (1952).

Russian secret police quartered in our house. This picture is the truth. It should be made. Only it is not strong enough."

I was beginning to feel the same way. We signed Krause (who did a fine job) and shooting started.

On the first day, some of the crew got hold of a radio. They translated for me: coming over the air was a list of the names of every member of the crew and of every German member of the cast including the circus people. It was a blacklist and a warning from Radio Leipzig: Quit – or else.

No one quit. But each one working understood the threat: when and if the Communists should take Bavaria, these men and women were marked. Naked calculated terror was being dispatched on the air above the barbed wire, the electrified wire, the mined fields of the boundary between East and West.

If you can put a date to such a thing, that was the moment when I understood and was committed to the picture I was making.

BABY DOLL

**Letters to
Tennessee
Williams –
undated extracts.**

Every man has had the experience of kidding around with a young girl and arousing feelings stronger than he's ready to deal with. The man gives it a whirl. The girl falls in love and, once aroused, pursues and wants more and more.

That is an essentially comic situation – I don't mean farcical, or even "funny" – but, by nature, comic.

Girls say: "Don't strike a match unless you can put out the fire."

Silva plays with Baby Doll – in the course of his investigation – and for the first time brings up water out of the well. It means an awful lot to her – the first time successful – and she's hungry for more of the same. But Silva is a young, ambitious businessman, terrifically competitive. He enjoys a roll on the nursery floor – but strictly *en passant*. But when this is done, it has no romantic swelling in his imagination. It is not LOVE. In fact he is just a little embarrassed by her holding on to him.

Karl Malden and Carroll
Baker in *Baby Doll* (1956).

June 8th, 1955

About our project, *Baby Doll*. I'm still planning to do it this fall and as early as possible. I would like to get Brando for it. I will carefully, but really carefully, consider Marilyn. Maybe she can do it. It's not impossible, but the main thing now is the script. Please send me what you have immediately. There really isn't a lot of time to waste if we are going to do it. There will be some back and forth on the script I know, and, if necessary, I can come to Europe for a visit at the end of the summer, but I will judge that when I get your material and see where you are . . .

A movie is so much more a collaborative business than a play and so much more is done pictorially. Anyway, you know all that.

God, I always feel when we talk together everything is clear in a matter of ten seconds. In fact, we have never had to talk much longer than that about any work problem because we always seem to be in immediate *rapport*. Even when we disagree we get each other's point so quickly . . .

There was a horrible story about William Inge, the author of *Splendor in the Grass*, having been told that he was sure to get the Pulitzer Prize, of his having prepared a party, food, invitations sent out, much liquor. Inge all dressed up, etc. The end was what you can imagine. Poor Bill.

Eli Wallach, Carroll Baker and Karl Malden in Baby Doll *(1956).*

Opposite: Carroll Baker and Eli Wallach in *Baby Doll* (1956).

ON "A FACE IN
THE CROWD"

Private notes
written on
January 4th,
1958, six months
after the film's
release.

A work of art should not show. It should not teach.

IT SHOULD BE.

It should be like a fact that has many meanings, all as complex and mixed up as life itself, contradictory, unfathomable, mysterious. The meanings should be there. But the audience should feel – as they do in the presence of a work of nature, that they have to find them, dig them out, and interpret them for themselves, each putting on each his own meaning.

We conceived *Face in the Crowd* as a "warning to the American people". This was the complete give away. The movie was conceived, written, directed and acted to show, to teach. Therefore it was oversimplified. It was mental. The complexity that we knew was left out. Above all we were out to show what a son of a bitch LR was – where we should have been showing that LR was us.

The big thing that would have made that story true and a piece of the contemporary scene would have been if LR at a point had reversed. If he had made the discovery: I am becoming a shit, this is not what I started out to do. I am no longer the master of my own destiny. They've got me. They've got me. I've got to get out. I've got to get out I've got to get out of it . . . AND THEN HE CANNOT.

Walter Matthau, Patricia Neal and Andy Griffith in *A Face in the Crowd* (1956).

112

Andy Griffith and Lee
Remick in *A Face in the
Crowd* (1956).

Andy Griffith in *A Face in the Crowd* (1956).

This would have been what would have happened to a human in that situation. But our fellow was a puppet designed to show what a son of a bitch he was. But the fact is more dangerous (bec. somebody "nice", like you is involved). And funnier and more complex, therefore more interesting.

And this contradictory set up, this inner conflict in a man, inner contradiction in a man, is the basis for real good story-telling because there is a back and forth play within a man that leads you to many, many incidents, and interesting unpredictable behavior under all different circumstances.

In other words it is life. It is a true story. The real LR is both good and bad.

This discovery and reversal are heart-breaking, recognizable. It is pain, within a soul.

And when you do this, your work of art is, it exists. It is not a contrivance, a contraption to teach.

Dear Bill: You once said: a first act should be written last. You meant when you had written it once and had written the rest of the play and knew where it was going and how it would end – then you *could* know what the first act should really be.

It was one of the really wise things I've ever heard said about playwriting.

I think it is a reference direct to *Splendor in the Grass*. If you take the climax of the first act as Bud's collapse, then shouldn't you not *rewrite* but reform the first act in a straight line to that point, to that climax. It isn't a matter of cutting, is it? It never is a matter of cutting really since you have to know *what to cut to*. Now we have much slighter but very damaging wandering. I'm speaking of the Ginny story. For a time the act is about Ginny with Bud and Deanie as *spectators*. You know that's bad.

I don't know how to solve this. But I know you'll find the solution to any problem you can see clearly as a problem.

What I was saying to you on the phone today was that Bud's collapse didn't come out of "not having his ashes hauled", sexual

Warren Beatty and Natalie Wood in *Splendor in the Grass* (1960).

frustration. There are several (for a "good" boy) terrible tensions that he is under. I think of him, at the beginning, as hero-worshipping Ace, admiring him enormously. For one thing he is caught between this emotion and the absolute thwarting of his emotional drive by Ace. He is spanning, or trying to, this conflict. Result: tension. Then there is the complication with Ginny. I feel somehow the Ginny story should become the Bud story. I don't know how (how much is direction or how much writing? I suspect mostly the latter) to do this. But that the collapse of Ginny brings about or helps bring about his own, that he plays the "scene" out with her, deeply and completely, is sure. Our thinking seems fuzzy here. Our thinking seems fuzzy re Bud's collapse altogether – therefore our first act is not firm.

Repeat: we are wonderful from about p.67 on (my script).

Yrs
GADGE[1]

[1]Gadge: Kazan's nickname in theatrical circles.

February 6th, 1960

117

A MAN FOR A PART

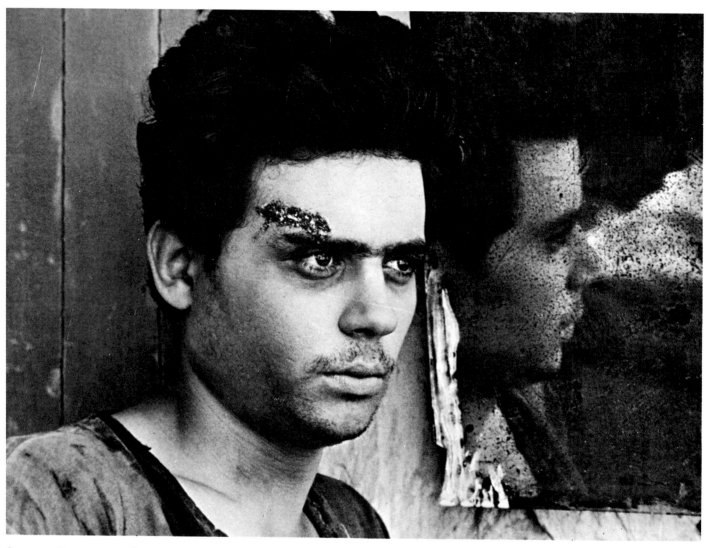

STATHIS GIALLELIS
AND "AMERICA
AMERICA"

*New York Herald
Tribune*
(December 8th,
1963).

My uncle was a gambler. My uncle is on my mind because I thought about him when I planned and wrote and made the picture *America America*. It is not his story, really, but it owes a lot to him. So do I. I probably would not be making pictures, nor be in America, if he had not, in a saga that is legendary in my family, contrived to get here. A. E. "Joe" Kazan, after he made his money (after he lost it, too), used to go to the racetrack every day. He'd wait for the right horse. Sometimes he'd lay only one bet all afternoon. He'd wait for a hunch.

The horses scare me. I don't bet. But when it comes to actors, perhaps I do the same thing: wait – and gamble.

All the time I was writing the book and planning the picture, I naturally had my eye out for an actor who could play the lead. I knew what I needed: a twenty-year-old boy who wasn't a boy, who was a man. I made a list, as I always do, of the qualities that the part, ideally, required. The actor should be (or seem) Greek "with eyes like moist olives", but of course he had to speak

Stathis Giallelis in *America America* (1964).

Elena Karam and Stathis Giallelis in *America America* (1964).

English. He should be home-spun, back-country, conscientious, dutiful, hungry, intense, unswerving. As always, I noted which was the most important of the needed qualities. It was the last. He had to be *unswerving*.

America America, which opens next Sunday in New York, is the story of a voyage. The boy makes his way against fantastic, overwhelming, preposterous odds. He makes it from his birthplace in Asia Minor to New York harbor. The year is 1896.

America is a dream, a rumor. He meets every kind of adventure and obstacle and hardship and setback. In the interior of Turkey, in the port of Constantinople (now Istanbul), even on the ship coming over, the voyage seems impossible. The key to the character, the quality without which the story could not happen, was persistence, doggedness, drive, unswervability.

When the time came, I looked for an actor in New York. Then I looked in California.

Then I started looking in dramatic schools all over, since the age I needed might be there. I found quite a few boys with talent, many with sensitivity. But on both coasts and in the places that I saw between them, I found either "nice guys" or the kind of surly adolescent that James Dean made famous. I didn't need either one. I couldn't use a "nice guy" who was anxious about being liked. I couldn't use a rebellious kid. For whatever reason, I could not find among these young American actors the drive, the fight I needed. None of these kids were going to strain themselves.

After a search in England, I had not found it either. I found a different kind of rebel. I found middle-class boys, hitting out at their fathers, at the Establishment, wallowing for the moment in the liberation of Bohemianism, while somewhere just below the surface was the breeding that willy-nilly imposed a kind of decorum. I couldn't use that, either.

Now I began to think of compromising my requirement of easy English. I went to France and there I found several most sensitive young actors. They read the script and responded to it well, talked very well indeed. But, basically, these boys believed in nothing: not in their country, not their society, certainly not in themselves. They were "cool", uncommitted – and precisely opposite to what I needed.

Shortly after, I was in Athens looking for locations and inspecting studio facilities. A colleague urged me to have a mass call for actors, if for no other reason, as a goodwill gesture. I agreed. The call went out, plainly specifying, "only for those who speak English". One hundred and fifty young actors jammed into the hotel. A few spoke English. Others were in the process of learning English. Others had intentions of one day taking a course in English. Still others knew they could learn English in a matter of weeks if it became necessary.

I hesitate to say in which category Stathis Giallelis belonged. I merely record that he caught my eye – physically, he was perfect for the part – and I asked him to read a scene for me in English. He replied (in Greek) that he had a bad cold and preferred not to. There was the assumption that this should satisfy me. I was quite sure he was lying. Questioning and investigation revealed that he had almost no acting experience. I decided to forget him and told him so. He was furious and demanded to read the script. It looked as if I might have difficulty getting him out of the hotel. He seemed to think I had an obligation to deal with him.

I had run head-on into the quality that I was searching for, but I didn't recognize it. Furthermore, I wasn't sure I liked it.

I promptly forgot Stathis Giallelis and continued my search elsewhere. I brought a young actor from France to New York to work on his English. He had every quality I needed – except the central one. I went to California a second time. I saw more boys, as before, brought up on cheeseburgers and milk shakes, not on goat's cheese and bitter olives.

Then I went back to Greece, this time to see if the country around Mount Olympus would serve for our mountain scenes. And there in the hotel lobby in Athens was this boy again, his eyes blazing half in hostility, half in hope, waiting for me as if his life hung on it.

He announced to me (in Greek) that he had learned English. He had done some work but, to be plain about it, he had not learned English. I told him again to stop hoping, that he was not going to get the part, that this was not a fairy story.

He did not stop hoping but he did relax a little. I listened to the story of his family. His father had been killed in the Greek civil war. He was now head of his family since he was the oldest male.

He took me to his home. At dinner, Stathis, twenty-one, sat at the head of the table,

Stathis Giallelis in *America America* (1964).

120

Stathis Giallelis and
Gregory Rozakis in
America America (1964).

waited on and looked up to by his widowed mother, his three sisters, his brother. The younger children took his guidance, his encouragement, his punishment – often manual. We all talked of civil war, of hunger, of penury, of the loyalty that grows in a family in desperate times. I looked at Stathis seated there. This boy, at twenty-one, had been through more than any American (or English or French) actor whom I had seen in two years of searching. He was not bland, not surly, not selfish, not indifferent, not uncommitted. He was a young, very tough, man.

After that evening at his home, I never got Stathis out of my mind. This time, I felt bad when I told him that I had no hope that he could learn English. I was trying to soften the blow when I said that if he spoke English – if he were in New York – it would be different.

One day three months later, he walked into my office on West 46th Street.

There is a story that he sold an acre of land that his father had left him on the Peloponnesus. There is a story that a quixotic friend lent him enough to fly to London. If so, then how he got from London to Idlewild is still a mystery. He explained the trip from Idlewild to Manhattan: it was achieved through the intercession of a friendly airline hostess. He had 44 cents in his pocket, but he was in my office in New York.

I looked at him and I thought, there he is – the real thing, on the hoof – like it or not. Unswerving! I can recognize a legend when I see one. At least the third time it walks up to me.

As I said, I wait and then, sometimes, I play hunches. He got the part, the long, difficult, crucial, leading part. And if he is, in the lingo of Hollywood, a "find", I cannot truthfully claim that I found him.

I can only say that I am very thankful that he found me and found his way into my picture.

"AMERICA AMERICA"

Lou Antonio in *America America* (1964).

America America. During the months and years I worked on this film, travelling through Europe looking for stories and locations and actors, I heard this phrase over and over and over until, it seemed to me, to have a meaning beyond the meaning of the two linked words. Titles often are what songs are – more than words – the sound of feeling!

America America. I heard it said longingly by a Greek peasant, a man who lived on a hillside, all of boulders, to which he carried his garden dirt in baskets slung over the back of his single donkey. I've heard the two words said as one by a Turkish official who, despite his high post in his own country, wanted desperately to come here. I've heard the paired words spat in venom by a French intellectual who, without knowing it, was paying us some inverted compliment through his scorn. I've heard the two words said in wonder and pleasure by the members of our Turkish motion-picture crew as they unpacked and inspected the camera equipment we brought to Istanbul. I've heard the words made into a doggerel song by gypsies camped just outside Athens who wanted me to be godfather to a new-born boy, thinking that by this connec-

tion with our country, however indirect, some good magic would result. I have also heard the title of my film come from the lips of an Italian carpenter, a member of my crew, who found that he and his fellow Italians were physically tougher than the American crew members and so saying that we were the standard to beat. And I've heard the phrase said by a famous Greek novelist who remembered Truman and recognized that if it hadn't been for an act of this country Greece would now be Communist and a part of the drab gray blanket which is Yugoslavia, Albania, Romania and Bulgaria.

But the memory I hold most dear in connection with my title is that of the Turkish peasant who lived in a little rock and reed village in the interior of Asia Minor, a place where people still use pancakes of animal dung for winter fuel, a proud gray man who had made many children, many fine kiddos whom I photographed one day all in a line. He later took me aside and brought me his favorite, apart from the others, and asked me to take this boy, patently so dear to him, back to this country, because, he thought, this one boy had something special and wonderful, something extra that wouldn't find growing space in his own village. And in attempting to describe what this one child had, he looked into the boy's face and said the phrase I use as title of my film.

Like it or not we are a dream. People hate us as well as love us. They point to our shortcomings and to the limitations of our "gadget culture", scoff and scorn, often with weight and some reason. But we are still a dream. We were in 1896 when my family came here looking for something. And we are now. Thousands and thousands still leave the stone mountains of Greece and the hot plateaux of Turkey in Asia. They go to Australia and they go to Ger-

America America (1964).

many. But if they are lucky they manage to get here. This is still the dream they choose if they can choose.

The book I wrote, *America America*, is about the longing and hunger of these people, and about what they will finally do to make their way here, endure any and all hardship, kill, even give up a piece of their essential pride and honor to achieve what we all here, now, take for granted.

There was one reaction I had to this book, again and again, an observation made not in criticism or praise, simply a basic reaction to the material. It was: "You've told the story of my own family." I've heard it from all nationalities, Greeks and Italians, Armenians, Russians post-revolution and pre-revolution, and lately the Iron Curtain refugees, the Bulgarians, Romanians, the Poles and the Czechs. I've heard "That's us!" from kids who sat, as I did, with their parents and heard, as I did, what must be the basic story of their family, the migration to this country. I heard "That is my family" from an actor in my film whose father, a Russian Jew, came here at the turn of the twentieth century. And I heard similar recognition from a lady I respect a lot, the Yankiest of the Yankees, whose family came here in the first big tide, mid-sixteen hundreds.

And I think, when you see the film, you will remember that we are all FROM somewhere, that we are all IMMIGRANTS and that we all came here LOOKING FOR SOMETHING. What is the responsibility of the dream to the dreamers? This is the story of this country.

Note written in 1963.

125

ON "THE ARRANGEMENT"

Extract from a letter to Michel Ciment, 1969.

My friends say of me that I enjoy being under attack, that I work most naturally with my back to the wall. Perhaps. I've certainly had a great deal of experience with films of mine that were slighted when they came out and then with the passing of time were seen in a warmer light.

The *New York Times* reviewing *America America* on the Sunday following its opening used the instance of the film simply as one illustration among others that there was a tendency current to allow films to run too long. No other substantial point was made by Mr Bosley Crowther about *America America*. The result: the film was labelled in people's minds simply as "too long". And that was that. Actually it did fairly well on its own for a few weeks, then unsupported, unacknowledged, it died.

Time has passed and now some people consider that film a classic. As they do *Viva Zapata!*, which also got no help from the critics here and none from its distributors. As with *A Face in the Crowd*, which did have its virtues recognized in moderation, while its faults were underscored to the point where again no successful effort could be made to sell it. As with *Baby Doll*, where Warner's simply did not dare to stand up to Cardinal Spellman's attacks. As with *Wild River*, which was hardly shown, anywhere; in France for instance only belatedly, after hysterical urging on my part and as an act of personal condescension.

So you see I've had some experience with people's backs, and I've had to learn to wait.

But I've never been attacked as viciously and as personally as I was on *The Arrangement*.

Why? This question is open. Was it the film they were attacking or me? If it was myself, that is not a matter for discussion. Prejudice cannot be treated rationally.

If it was the film, I would want to make a few points on its behalf and for its understanding.

The Arrangement has faults; it has my own deficiencies. But must we not measure works in the field of art by their virtues? The only perfect film I may have made was a "chase", and it was only perfect, if it was, because it was perfectly mechanical. As soon as you begin to deal in ambivalences and in symbols of any complexity and as soon as you begin to offer personal attitudes and views, you risk misunderstanding. And rejection.

The Arrangement is not autobiographical in its plot but its values are as I see them. And its purpose is not the conventional one: to entertain.

The Arrangement was made to disturb people.

To this end, the personages depicted are not individual; they are prototypes.

They were intended to be the social masks of our day and of our country in our day.

Florence, the wife, for instance, is the typical upper-middle-class wife. Her typicality is her tragedy. She has all the standards, values and aspirations, all the virtues too, of the upper-middle-class wife. She wants to do good; her good intentions kill her and her husband. She is above all a class product, predetermined by her social training. She is an epitome.

Eddie, the central figure, is also a prototype. His character split, the "divided self", is classic. He wants to be a success but he wants to be a rebel. He aspires to be a typical American and yet he is inevitably an outsider. He wants to be commercial and he wants to be someway "artistic". He wants a secure domestic situation and he wants to be sexually free. He wants to be able to pose as a situation requires, and he wants to be true to himself. He has two careers, pursued simultaneously. And he has three names, a different one for each side of him.

Faye Dunaway in *The Arrangement* (1969).

E. J. André, Richard
Boone and Anne Hegira in
The Arrangement (1969).

I was trying to deal with conceptual beings, not heroes and heroines.

This seems to me, at the moment, to be the most effective and true way to describe our social scene. In that sense *The Arrangement* is the most social film I have made.

It does not seem valuable to me to photograph the demonstrators massed outside the Conrad Hilton, or fighting the police in Lincoln Park summer before last, without doing something more: looking beneath their beards and beads and under their blanket rolls and recognizing them for what they are, the well-educated children of middle-class America. And devout idealists. To show them simply as rioters or eccentrics or even revolutionaries is to enforce a false impression.

I even think it's dangerous and ignorant to pass off the police as themselves rioters (which they were) and "pigs" without indicating something of what they are in class, in education, in ideals. To simply dismiss them as sadists doesn't increase our knowledge of them or of our country and time.

In this light, most "social" films seem to me to evade the problem they profess to attack.

Many of them – so say their makers – are metaphors. They are "Westerns" for instance and their heroes are outlaws, sheriffs and cowboys. But, say their authors, they are really about Vietnam and why we're there, or about the prevalence and dangers of violence or perhaps about neo-McCarthyisms.

Kirk Douglas, Michael
Higgins and Deborah Kerr
in *The Arrangement*
(1969).

Or they are about hippies, gentle and cute or eccentric and violently alienated, or about urban derelicts, or about simple Italian peasants getting the better of the German Wehrmacht or what not. All metaphors!

But the audience sits there, enjoying the show or not enjoying the show, and its content and social meaning passes through them like morning coffee. Those are *those other fellows* they say. What that film seems to be saying is not about us. Of course it's true! Violence is terrible. The Nazis were monsters as well as finally stupid. Forty-Second Street is a terrible place – but very colorful.

But how does that apply to us? It doesn't. It's only about those freaks, those Wild West characters, about Nazis, about Italian peasants, about those depraved derelicts, about those other people, those special characters. Not about us!!

One critic said *The Arrangement* embarrassed her. Which was exactly what I intended. I did wonder how she could have been embarrassed at what she saw in my film and not embarrassed by what she saw in many other films she has looked at this season. The answer, I'm afraid, is that the "sordid" events in other films (incidentally far more luridly portrayed) were happening to people from whom she could separate herself, or to put it more bluntly, whom she could patronize. Yes, those awful things do happen among derelicts on Forty-Second Street, or (safely) in the past, or among low life of other countries. But when they happen in the homes of people of the same culture and of the same class as herself, they embarrass. Well, they should.

129

Faye Dunaway in *The Arrangement* (1969).

an individual. She is *The Perfect Wife*, a living prototype. This is not actually the way Miss Kerr herself is; she is a charming and true woman. But I believed that the image she spent so many years building on the screen (often against her will) was in this case operating for me.

And so Eddie Anderson. Kirk is one of our bravest leading men; he has never lost a screen war, rarely a battle. He is one of a group of leading men who are the filmic symbols of our national invincibility. What do I now show? That this prototype, who has always reassured us, is in deep trouble, actually at the end of a road.

And so with the other figures: the immigrant father who came to America to be free to make a fortune, the girl-friend prototype of the pill revolution, the lawyer, fair and friendly and completely "standard", who ironically wins it all in the end.

And the climax of my film simply says that our society condemns a man who breaks the mould as erratic and finally dangerous, and therefore in one way or another restrains him. In this case within an institution for the mentally deranged. And who puts him away? His best friend, the lawyer and his dearly beloved wife! And why? *For his own good!*

That is what the film is about. You will notice that no one in it is entirely likeable and no one is entirely unlikeable. No one triumphs. The end too is uncertain. People simply break apart and go in opposite directions. It's what's happening in this country.

I'm forced to add "As I see it". I don't think many others here did. Of course I wonder if this is not my fault. But I also wonder if the film should not have been judged by those whose profession it is to entertain their readers by judging a film by what it was attempting – as well as by what it achieved.

I do not think the film is behind the times or, as some of the New York critics said, old-fashioned. It is ahead of its times, but not in its techniques. There isn't a shot in

I tried to make a film where the people on the screen are the epitomization of the people watching the screen. I tried to make everything as familiar and as typical as possible. I accepted the danger of banality. But above all I wanted the audience to jump a little, yes, to be embarrassed, to see themselves and ask: is that what makes me tick too? Are those my own standards? My values? Is that my situation? Is that the truth about me?

And so – I suppose inevitably – "It can't be! Fuck Kazan!"

But for an instant the people in the audience may have asked the real questions.

I believe that now, in this time and in this situation, films should talk, particularly to Americans, but to your people as well, *without allowing them an exit*! They must not be able to say, "That's about those other fellows," or "That's that very special case," or "Those are *exceptional* people!"

They must not be able to patronize what's on the screen. They must not be able to escape the inferences of what's shown them.

I wanted my film to seem at first perfectly familiar. Which is one of the reasons I cast the film as I did. For instance Deborah Kerr can no longer quite be, on the screen,

the film made with a zoom lens. There are no long tracking shots of people on motorbikes and none of people seeming to run in place because they were photographed with a long lens.

Its novelty, a genuine one I think, was to make the personages UN-special. In the effort to say to the audience: That is you, like it or not, that dilemma is yours, accept it or not; that crisis is yours, turn away if you can!

One final oddity: many of the reviewers, in noticing the film, really reviewed my book. When the book came out in 1966 the *New York Times* reviewed it twice. One review was worse than the other. The man who wrote for their Sunday book supplement referred to my book as garbage. Nevertheless it was number one bestseller for forty-two weeks. Murder having failed once, they struck again with all the ferocity of the intellectual beast who has missed a killer.

I believe this time, in America, they will succeed. But I don't believe they will in Europe; I stand in the hope that people there will understand what I tried to do, and value it. And in time, perhaps everywhere. The other day I was told that the critic for *L'Humanité* had finally been taken to see *Wild River* by Bertrand Tavernier and he had liked it very much. If that kind of a miracle can happen, anything can.

Kirk Douglas and Deborah Kerr in *The Arrangement* (1969).

THE CINEMA IN AMERICA

Lecture given on May 7th, 1971, at Wesleyan University, to which Elia Kazan had donated his archives.

Over the years I've come to have great suspicion of absolutes. Men whose profession it is to be right cock my trigger. This goes, of course, for critics but perhaps most for lawyers. What is a lawyer, I wonder, when he's not right? President Nixon, you'll recall, is a lawyer, so it cannot possibly occur to him what a glorious place he'd have in history if he'd admit for all of us that we've made a ghastly, shameful error.

What I said about people whose profession it is to be right applies, of course, to teachers.

Now that I have your full and undivided attention, I will proceed.

No, I am not going to take pot shots at the members of the academic community. Residual loyalty, I suppose. I used to be one. I was twenty-four years old and taught a class in the basic theories of directing in the Stanislavsky method. My auspices was an organization called the New Theatre League. This was in the 1930s, in the good old "The Theatre is a Weapon" days and I not only taught there, I was on the Praesidium – which is what a more modest organization like US Steel calls a Board of Directors. I was one of the guiding theoreticians in what we called the leading cadre. Our planning sessions arrived at absolutely clear – and rigid – postures through a process known as socialist criticism. We raised a lot of mean hell with each other in those socialist criticism sessions. But when conclusions were reached and new directives hammered out, there was no more questioning – until the next session of socialist criticism.

I was in perfect concert with all this. I was absolutely sure of everything in those days, had everything set in my mind and I use the word "set" as in a reference to concrete. One of Karl Marx's finest sayings was "Doubt everything". I and my friends must have overlooked the passage in which those two words appear because to doubt we were strangers. I knew the laws of directing for the stage and I laid them on my class with a heavy trowel. My pupils were men between twenty-five and fifty-five – I was always the youngest person in that classroom, but that didn't bother me a bit. Attendance varied depending on what "Actions" were going on that day. Part of the training for agit-prop theatre – Theatre the Weapon – was to picket and to speak on street corners. I still don't put that down.

Things were a lot simpler and a lot clearer then. A play had a lesson to teach and that theme was to be dramatized in an event which dominated the third act. Everything before was chosen to lead up to that climactic event. This law, unity through climax, was most clearly enunciated by a man named John Howard Lawson; it still has considerable value. Until you think of the playwrights it excludes.

Contrast the basic theory of Broadway play-making of that time. It was laid down by Howard Lindsay – he wrote, directed and starred in *Life with Father*, you other gray-hairs will remember – and his basic law was: organize the audience's emotions. George Abbot, another giant of that time, elaborated this as follows. Act One: get them to love your hero, then get him up a tree. Act Two: throw stones at him. Act Three: get him down. It was important to make the audience quickly dislike the "heavy". One of the best ways to do this was to show him kicking a dog. Figuratively.

Well, we at the New Theatre League were pretty scornful of all that. We wanted to disorganize the audience's emotions, *discredit* their heroes, keep them *up* that tree, make the audience feel as they were *not prepared* to feel, upset their values, disturb their composure, disembowel their prejudices, spill them out and leave the middle-class audience no reason for believing in themselves. This was all pre-Artaud.

I must admit I still tend to think that way.

Kirk Douglas in *The Arrangement* (1969).

I used to prepare each Tuesday's class riding downtown in the subway. It took me every bit of the twenty minutes' ride from where I lived. Now it would take me a good nine months' hard labor to prepare a course in directing that I'd respect. And at that I'd probably want to postpone the first class.

Which leads me to this occasion.

When Wyman[1] first approached me about being here with you, I told him I was working frantically on a long and sometimes boring novel and that I was desperate to finish so I could begin to edit it. I didn't have the time, I told him, to speak anywhere on anything. But Wyman, as you must know, is a beguiling man and in very short order I found myself committed to what we agreed to call an informal chat. [Hold up manuscript.]

I got a handsomely printed announcement and there was nothing informal about it, was there? Then followed a charming note from a lady: would I come to dinner afterwards she asked – an invitation that I was delighted to accept. She concluded by saying that she was looking forward to my presentation. Now that word – presentation – that's a heavy word to lay on a man; I decided then and there I'd better type this up.

On the inscribed invitation the subject is announced to be THE FILM IN AMERICA. I do have a way of leaping into the middle of my subject, don't I?

THE FILM IN AMERICA. Well, why not? It's as good a title as any. I've been noticing that as a man gets older, all subjects blend into each other. Norman Mailer, writing about the moon shot, begins by complaining that he wasn't asked to comment on the death of Ernest Hemingway and ends by inviting you to wonder with him why his wife Beverly left him. He explains neither irrelevancy so perhaps you may begin to see that everything is after all related to everything else. As he wonders about it all, the reader does too.

Whatever else you may say about Mailer, you must admit *he was there*! Whatever he describes, he was into first hand. Inviting you to share his troubles and his concerns, he makes nothing easy for you as he makes nothing easy for himself. He irons out no contradictions, rather seeks them; they fascinate him. Perhaps he wants to leave you with the feeling that the most profound intellectual and psychic state is one of informed bewilderment, therefore of searching. That is the state in which he lives.

What can a man do rightly, perfectly, except be witness to his own experiences and report them as honestly as he can? That is the word many French aesthetes use to refer to the artist. Witness. A witness to his times. The artist reports on the history of his day as it runs through his life. That is what he truly knows: what happened, what is happening to him. That is what he can honestly tell you about. The rest is dubious material; it is for the critics. Absolutes change with the fashions.

I have always thought that the highest form of literature is confession – whether somewhat disguised as in the novels of Dostoevsky and Flaubert and Dreiser and Tolstoy or more directly stated as in the music of Beethoven and Bessie Smith or quite plainly put as in the best last plays of O'Neill and the best first plays of Tennessee Williams.

So I do not come before you now to theorize about the film in America, to sell you a viewpoint, my interpretation, to impose my order on it. That, as I say, is for critics.

I can only tell you what happened to me, tell you how the past, the present and the future of the film in America might to some small degree be revealed by my own recent history. And if what should be concluded is not always clear to you as I talk, it's because I eschew the word "should" and because I'm still in process and don't see my way too far ahead.

One more story and then I'll start.

One of my good friends is Boris Aronson, the scene designer. I see him rarely today since I have lost most of my interest in the theatre. But I used to see him often on opening nights. On one such occasion, I

[1] Wyman W. Parker, the Wesleyan librarian.

encountered him coming up the aisle after the first act. "Well, Boris," I said, "how do you like it?" "Marvelous," he answered in his rich Russian lisp, "it's tho confuthed!" After the second act I sought him out. "And now, Boris," I asked, "how do you like it now?" "Not so good," he answered, "it's clearing up."

The last few years of my life in films has been extremely disparate – and, at the same time, quite related. And, to tell you the precise truth, I've thought them glorious. Perhaps not in achievement, certainly not in critical acclaim, but in experience? Wild!

It all started in 1966. I had lost interest in the theatre at the same time many of the playwrights whose plays I used to direct lost most of their interest in it.

The death of my wife – with whom I started out in the Group Theatre in 1932 – seemed to declare some sort of stop on that part of my life.

I had never written a book, always wished I had been a writer, but never believed myself able that way. But simply out of desire to understand what had been happening to me, I began to write down what you might call letters to myself, confessions.

The fact that *The Arrangement* became a bestseller was a total surprise to me. The fact that it was number one on the *Times* list for thirty-four weeks I still don't believe.

The money, the attention, the praise, even the huckstering since I had never done it before, were very pleasant indeed. I enjoyed them all.

But the great thing about the experience was my realization that I could now embark on a second life. When has man not wanted that, to be someway born again? And there was this further good news: that my work from now on might come out of my own belly.

I immediately began to plan a program of more writing. I had actually started another book – when an unexpected thing happened.

Faye Dunaway in *The Arrangement* (1969).

I began to get offers from a film company for my property. Property. Note that word. Remember I did not write the book for a film, did not believe as I wrote it that it would make a film. Now it was a property. I still doubted it would make a good film.

The offers of purchase moneys were large. It was also suggested to me that they could be spread out over ten years. The carrot dangled in front of me was a ten-year subsidy.

A living in the performing arts is precarious, tenure (you've heard that word before), tenure is uncertain, cost of living, children, a second wife, a second family, love of travel, books, country living, all, all came very, very high. And there was the oldest dread I had: that I might sometime be forced to do work I abominated just to pay the bills. I've done my share of poor work but not ever for those reasons.

Besides I still loved films, wanted to make more. And now – one of my own! Why not?

And since I was doing it, instructions to my negotiator to make the damnedest deal he could. He did just that.

Now what happens when a film is identified by its high purchase price as a BIG picture?

Everything must be done to ensure its commercial success.

The purchase price becomes the bench mark by which all expenditures are measured.

Lots of money must be spent to protect lots of money.

All determining criteria are those of commerce.

The financing and distributing company wanted stars.

I saw some sense in this wish – since my story's central characters are all in their middle forties – or over. I have always preferred working with "unknowns" but if a professional actor reaches forty-five and is still unknown something pretty serious is wrong. My discoveries were all young people – when I discovered them. This was not the occasion for another "discovery".

I tried for a middle ground, reaching for Marlon Brando, then discredited, marked down, "not bankable". I ended up with Kirk Douglas. Bankable.

Wanting Barbara Loden, I ended up with Faye Dunaway.

I found Kirk most intelligent, devoted, professional, ambitious. I knew Faye as a sensitive and gifted person. I have no complaint to make of either.

Except scale. I was in Hollywood.

What is that – Hollywood? In a capsule: it's art organized as an industry.

So what happens?

An extra day's work with Faye – a girl I had discovered in an audition for Lincoln Center Repertory Company and so launched on her way – would cost me, I think we found, about sixty-six hundred dollars. A day!

Kirk's suits – well I won't be able to shock you with the exact figure because I've forgotten it, my mind protects itself by forgetting – but I do remember it was in four figures. Apiece!

The housecoat that Deborah Kerr wore in one scene on one day was also well into four figures.

A small apron? Three hundred-odd dollars, very odd.

Added to each figure was something called Studio Overhead which swelled every item by a third.

The money was flying in every direction.

It was melon-cutting time.

I had never done a film before that cost a fourth of what this one cost.

Still, there it was, I had set the scale.

I had launched that orgy of spending.

So shut up and get on with it!

And worst of all – precisely because everything, sets, costumes, the large crew, the expensive talent, the tiniest knick-knack was so expensive – time was at a premium, I'm talking about working time.

You may not know – but you will easily understand – why time is, of everything the producer can provide the director, the thing he values most. Time to rehearse, time to experiment a little, time to reverse his field, time to get the actors really going – and time on another, later day to do a scene over – this kind of time, this use of time, was not there.

I was working in the film industry and not in films as expression.

Things were topsy-turvy.

There was something else being lost,

something I wasn't able to immediately analyse, saw clearly only later.

Modesty. The scale of human affairs, the small arena of the single human psyche. *That* was being swamped, the privacy of private problem. In short, the scale of humanity.

I had not, after all, written an earth-shattering book. What merits it had were those of my efforts to face my very personal, very inner experiences. Personal, not epic. The people I wrote about were not important people – they were only important to the author. The people I wrote about were not glamorous people. They were not even that good looking. They were, all in all, nothing much. Their problems were not in scale with that kind of cast, and that kind of budget.

I wrote a book to disturb people to make them question themselves. The industry manufactures entertainment that everyone must like, it must offend no one, everyone must want to go. Everyone who goes must be pleased!!

When the film was finished, the people who financed it hated it. This was a surprise to them. It was as though they had never read the book – only the little weekly ladder of success in the Book Review Section of the *Sunday Times*.

There is a final irony. The man in the company most instrumental in getting them to put up $6 million eight hundred thousand dollars – that's what it cost – had not, in fact, read the book. He had a copy, autographed by the author, he had smelled into it, even started it, but – as he told me frankly – he does not read. Not books.

Actually, I differed from the critics. I thought the film a failure, yes, but still – a success. Imperfect – I valued it. The French critics – known to be eccentric or ahead of their time – they too praised it. But it was not anything like it should have been, or could have been.

I was far out on the wrong road, I had to face that. I had someway betrayed myself.

I made a discovery – that money is the root of all evil. Not original with me? Right! We keep learning the same lessons over and over.

The Greeks have a saying, hard to translate: "Good things you learn at once, bad things you must learn twice." To learn twice was my destiny.

It had been the desire of Budd Schulberg and myself for nearly fifteen years to make a film about Puerto Ricans in the United States.

While I was making the film *The Arrangement*, while I still had the status and commercial heft of a best-selling author, Budd and I were able to persuade a film company to buy on our behalf the film rights to two books. One, a National Book Award winner, Oscar Lewis's *La Vida*, and the other an excellent, true book by Piri Thomas, *Down These Mean Streets*, which dealt with the Puerto Ricans who lived in New York City's El Barrio.

In light of later events – the film is not yet made – I have wondered whether the people who put up the money to buy that material read it. Did the executives who were busy those months frantically cutting cost losses in the millions by lopping off secretarial personnel, did they read the books they bought for us?

Because a year later when they read *In the Streets*, the screenplay Budd Schulberg made from this material, they seemed surprised to learn that the story was the odyssey of a Puerto Rican family through the world of brown poverty, surprised to find that the story was not a totally heartening one, in fact more a warning than a candidate for the late show.

A couple of experienced fellows Budd and I are, but still we were shocked by the speed with which our project was dropped by the company originally interested. And then turned down by absolutely every other company in the business.

We don't give up easily. *On the Waterfront* was also turned down by every company in the business – Darryl Zanuck put it most succinctly when he refused that film: "Who gives a shit about Labor unions?" he said – and it was finally produced by Sam Spiegel who was too discredited to get anything better.

But nobody would go on this one.

I told Budd it was the budget, the budget was too high at three million four hundred thousand. We began to chop into it. But it was too high at two two, I'm talking about millions, too high at one five, too high at one, and by that time we were offering to work at zero dollars salary, ready, in fact, to do anything, just to not suffer the final indignity, just out of a determination that *In the Streets* should NOT NOT be made.

But we got nowhere, still haven't, are still trying, but still nowhere.[2] Is it the brown poverty part of it? Is it primarily the cost? Whatever it is we have to admit, Budd and I, the kind of picture we have made in the past is not being made today, not readily, well, not at all.

The last straw in my own feelings was a perfectly trivial incident. The executive officer of a company for whom a film of mine fifteen years before had made many millions did not return my phone calls. For two days I waited for a word from him. No answer. Finally I had to call an underling to get the news that this company was still, on the third submission, on the no-salary budget, still not the least interested.

I began to feel like a Dreiser character, Hurstwood at the end of *Sister Carrie*. I was in a deep pot hole at the end of a well-bombed road. I was up against it.

Greeks are resilient. While the war to decide to show or ignore Puerto Rican pov-

erty was being fought out, I was preparing something else, a film with my wife, Barbara.

Wanda. The story was Barbara's idea. While I helped her rough out the screenplay, in all essentials, it's hers.

We organized together a Foundation for Film-makers, a non-profit-making corporation whose legally stated purpose was to produce films that couldn't be otherwise done and that we wanted to do. And of course to produce them at an extremely low figure.

The original plan was for me to direct *Wanda* and that it be made underground.

The word underground, applied to films, means several things but it always means one particular thing, that the film is to be made with a very small crew and that this crew be *not* necessarily members of the IATSE, the International Alliance of Theatrical Stage Employees.

Being, what I am, a child of the 1930s, I hesitated about making a non-union film, just as I would about crossing a picket line no matter what I thought of the union picketing.

So I consulted a lawyer and he called a luncheon meeting with two officers of the NY local of the IATSE at which Barbara and I were present and at which I did make a presentation; we wanted what are known as "concessions".

I told these two men that we could only make our film at a budget that made it impossible to operate in the traditional way. Perhaps it was time to take a new look. Times had changed – witness my recent experience with the Puerto Rican project. I asked their permission to make the film with a crew of seven or eight at the most and to avoid the expenses of such useless departments as wardrobe, hairdressing, make-up and unit publicity, that furthermore how many men worked was to

2The project never materialized.

138

Barbara Loden in her own film, *Wanda* (1970).

be determined by us, not by them, by actual need, not by the necessity of keeping full union membership employed.

It was a cordial lunch; the food was OK.

I waited for an answer.

I got none.

Well, that's not accurate. I got none for many, many weeks. By which time we were well into making the film.

The answer when it did come was no.

Meantime we had proceeded. Determined to keep the faith as I had been brought up to believe in it, I had urged and finally convinced Barbara to direct the film herself, assuring her that I'd stand right behind her at all times, ready when she needed help. About union permission Barbara was a realist.

Well, it turned out to be a blessing. Barbara did not need much help and none on essentials. She showed herself to be an excellent director and has since received all the praise she deserved for that. I helped

some, around the edges, but, as the days passed, less and less until, finally, not at all. I stayed home and worked on my book mornings, and swam with the kids in the afternoons. I babysat, while she made *Wanda*. Women's Lib please note.

It turned out that what I had told the IATSE officers was precisely true. *Wanda* cost $135,000. We could not have raised more. And couldn't now, after all the acclaim. The sad truth is that with all the fine things said about the film here, in England, in San Francisco, at Venice, it has done very poor business.

Still, who would say that *Wanda* should not have been made?

Obviously commercial criteria – especially those determined on a scale of operation that is no longer realistic – should not determine what films are NOT made or even, to judge from the recent past, what films ARE made.

So now I had to face the elemental facts. I was not going to be able to make the films I wanted to make, not in the old way, not in this time of an industry that was dying and desperately trying to find a way to revive itself.

I'd have to learn the lessons of *The Arrangement*, of *In the Streets*, of *Wanda*. I'd have to find a new road for myself. And perhaps for others like me.

Patrick McVey in *The Visitors* (1971).

140

If I didn't, I'd have to suffer silence. Silence for an artist is death – the same thing.

I won't tell you my processes of thought, I'll only tell you what I did.

I live in Newtown, Connecticut on a piece of land where there are two houses. I live in one and my son Chris, a writer, lives in the other with his wife and young son.

One day I said three sentences to him. A story, a suggestion for a film that could be made entirely on our place quickly while the snow was on the ground, using the two houses, only five actors, a crew even smaller than the one which made *Wanda* at a cost lower too.

Non-union.

I still felt nervous about that. But there was no choice, that or silence. Or that other possibility: making the kind of film I didn't want to make.

My son Chris went for it. In three weeks he had written the script. He called it *Home Free*.[3] We spent another couple of weeks working it over. Then we proceeded. I took no director's fee. The crew was cameraman and three others. They were excellent, all four. Of the five actors, three had never worked before, one was just beginning what will be a fine career and the last, an older man, is a refugee. From where? From Hollywood.

All the five actors worked at minimum Screen Actors' Guild rates. Decent salaries – not foolish. The cameraman and the

Patricia Joyce and Chico Martinez in *The Visitors* (1971).

[3]Original title of *The Visitors*.

141

Patrick McVey and Steve Railsback in *The Visitors* (1971).

crew were well paid; they could be since they were only four.

The work was a delight. The root Latin word for amateur means to love. This was an amateur production, I was an amateur again. I couldn't wait to get to work every morning. After all the years!

I never hurried. Running costs were low so I realized my ambition. Every time I didn't like the way a scene turned out, I did it over. That is a luxury I never had on that six million eight hundred thousand dollar film, *The Arrangement*.

Oh, the cost! When we finished the principal photography of *Home Free* we had spent an amount precisely equal to the money Faye Dunaway's agent took from her salary for his services to her on *The Arrangement*.

Something was trying to tell me something!

I started in films in 1934 as a documentary film-maker. I was back carrying a tripod again – doing "everything" – and I liked it.

Well, that is it. The film in America, its

recent history as seen through the experience of one man.

That's where I am now – at this point in my moon shot.

Will it go on the same way? What does?

I don't know where we're heading. Or where I am.

One immediate contradiction, for instance. I like to see expensive pictures, I like big scenes, big battles, I like the steps of Odessa in *Potemkin* and the great crowds of *Intolerance*, I like to deal with that kind of excitement as I did in Budd Schulberg's *A Face in the Crowd*, I like to see fine actors like those in *The Rules of the Game*, I like the gilt edges of the films of Ernst Lubitsch, they weren't made on tight budgets, I like all that, elaborate costumes, luscious scenery, great music, fantasy, I like Ken Russell and the Near-East hordes rushing at each other in *Lawrence of Arabia*. I like going far out on distant locations to make films, I like to see another John Ford in Monument Valley doing impractical things arrogantly, I want big films to go on, even bigger films, and I hope to make films of that kind myself – that's what the money's for – to be squandered.

Another complexity. The unions are right. Fine experienced technicians who've spent their lives doing their part deserve the security of a reliable living wage and they're going to get it.

So what's the answer?

I don't know.

Clearly we need – we, the community of film-makers – to have one hell of a session of socialist criticisms. We need to look together at the new situation, find and make a fresh start.

But as we wait for that to happen, I must admit considerable personal relief. I've found, for the time, one way to keep going. I've not been silenced.

142

NOTES ON MONROE STAHR IN "THE LAST TYCOON"

December 20th, 1974

Monroe learned years ago that if he showed a weakness of any kind he would be devoured. And the truth is he would be.

So he has donned this invulnerable coat of steel. There isn't an aperture that any weapon can penetrate. He cannot be fazed. He sees the power struggle and sees who his enemies are. He gives them the greatest defense of all, a pleasant front. Always polite, always plain and clear and professional. He doesn't like any of them because to like one would allow himself to be taken. Nor is he impolite or rude to them. He is impersonal. If he were to show his distrust or occasionally antagonism it would give them a chance to hit back at him, it would justify their bad attitudes towards him.

But the result of all this is that he has a terrible need for tenderness and love. Since he was not and cannot express or exercise any of it, he is loaded down with desire, not for fucking, but for love. He then loves excessively. And at the same time that he is feeling this extreme desire for closeness, he is aware of its dangers. *It leaves him vulnerable* to hurt. So he keeps trying to rein himself in, he keeps reconsidering. Does he want to go that far, does he want to expose himself to hurt that much, does he want to take off his coat of mail?

The part of the script that worries me most is not the big scenes nor the psychological scenes. These are comparatively simple. What worries me is the love scene in the middle, particularly the scenes where Pinter has suggested nudity. This is so banal by now. Who wants to be diverted by genitalia? That is not what the story is about. The love in this story is need for closeness and tenderness. It is stored-up goodness and love hunger. On both sides. The tragedy is that they could be wonderful together and they can't quite make it because of his nature and because of the circumstance she brings with her and because of her need for a man who is not a "KING", for a safe, simple, good, reliable man.

January 5th, 1975

Stahr is special, unique, monastic, a relic.

He walks alone. Occasionally men follow him waiting for orders.

Dana Andrews and Robert De Niro in *The Last Tycoon* (1976).

During the preparation for the shooting of The Last Tycoon *Elia Kazan kept a regular record, part personal diary, part work in progress. These notes (several hundred pages) were never intended for publication. They helped the director to work out his film, and at the same time to survive a particularly painful time in his life (his mother was dying in Los Angeles, a few steps away from the studio). Here are a few notes on the character of Monroe Stahr.*

143

Robert De Niro and Tony Curtis in *The Last Tycoon* (1976).

Robert De Niro and Ingrid Boulting in *The Last Tycoon* (1976).

He is in a daze of work and thought. He carries the whole studio operation in his head. And he wants it that way.

Zanuck was a tycoon too. He walked alone. He had nothing on his mind except business, the business of the studio operating! Only his relationship to women was different. But it was the same coin, other side. That generation divided women into whores and saints. Stahr–Edna vs Kathleen. Zanuck, remember.

He has a vision of a perfect life and he operates from it. It's the only way he can. But the studio can't operate that way anymore and the writers can't and won't and women aren't that way anymore. Even Kathleen. She reads his hesitation right.

How? She knows that something is making him hesitate and she also knows that if it ever came down to a choice, he'd choose the studio, its operation. The movies are him. When he says, "I don't want to lose you!" it means the studio as well as Kathleen and perhaps the studio above all.

February 19th, 1975

Spiegel is concerned that I will "sentimentalize" Stahr. He keeps reminding me, every time I discuss it with him, that Stahr is ruthless. Yesterday he said, he has a tendency to be power mad, or that he is. I've forgotten which distinction he made. I have thought about his point and it has a certain validity. Stahr should be awful tough, "that little tin Vine Street Jesus". Perhaps it is necessary for a young man –

Ray Milland, Robert Mitchum, Jeanne Moreau and Robert De Niro in *The Last Tycoon* (1976).

Kubrik, for instance – to be ruthless when he comes to power so young. He has to command elders and he can't help thinking that they resent his authority over them. And that he also develops a taste for it since he is and has been right so often and they have been wrong so often. And it is inevitable that he soon gets trapped in this power, that he enjoys it, that it becomes habitual with him. AT THE SAME TIME, I have worked with Zanuck and although he certainly enjoyed his power and while he was a "boy wonder" and while he ran the studio with an absoluteness that was overwhelming, nevertheless he "came on" like a regular guy. He only acted all-powerful when he was challenged. And even then he didn't yell. He simply became unequivocal and somewhat steely. And he might wave his arms and reject challenge or qualification. Spiegel himself is a tycoon of this sort and he certainly has a taste for power, but he comes on like a Dutch uncle and is also full of a kind of charming schmaltz and generosity and intelligence. He wants to be both, a human and an all-powerful tycoon at the same time, which "bothness" is Stahr's problem at this period, it seems to me. Earlier on, he had to develop an iron front, an unwavering toughness because he was a kid making adults take his orders. Cf. Billy Martin and the Texas Rangers. But after

his wife's death something happened to him and he feels that he has frozen his heart and abandoned his humanity and has no warmth left and he begins this effort that defeats and tumbles him down, the effort to regain his humanity.

He is a hard-nosed businessman. He is precise and exact and most knowledgeable about his business actions. He is ruthless. He sees things in a clear balanced light. But when he first sees Kathleen it is in a strange refracted light, twice reflected, that is, from the big units on stands that are rushed in to light the flood. And when he sees her in this light, she seems to be floating in the water. The upper half of her body is lit and the bottom half is not lit, so she is ethereal and floats in space. The wind is blowing her hair, which makes her seem even more romantic and unreal and visionary. And when Stahr sees Kathleen the second time, he sees her just out of the door of the house where she lives. There is an arbor, a shallow one, but covered with leaves, etc., in front of the door, and the light is mottled and soft and the effect again is a romantic and unreal and visionary one. She looks like a spirit self-illuminated from within. And her face has a soft light that is tinted green and yellow. And when Stahr

THE AMBIVALENCE OF STAHR

Robert De Niro, Theresa Russell and Jack Nicholson in *The Last Tycoon* (1976).

sees her in the parking light, again the lighting should make her a vision. And just before at the party, the lights should be colored and soft and she should be a romantic vision. And when they make love in the house, they are lit when they are lit (not the first time, that is twilight; not the second, that is moonlight) by a yellow candle and a red heater's light, etc. She is always a dream figure, an *apparition*, an ideal of beauty and romance, never a hard, plain, realistic image. So KATHLEEN should always be presented with a mystery about her, suggesting always more than the literal, a phantom, a dream, a romantic projection of Stahr's need for that. The first time in a sudden swing of a beam that penetrates and disrobes her, leaves her transparent as a Morris Graves bird, disrobing her, making her into a ghostly figure. The wind that follows an earthquake helps. The second time in the mottled mystery of the light of an arbor before her door. She doesn't come out of that soft mysterious light until Edna goes. Then she steps forward. Again a light from behind puts her in an aura.

Kathleen must always be apparitional.

Monroe Stahr has a sense of nobility and a sense of mission that promise us a tragedy.

De Niro has to characterize Stahr this way. *He is a young king*, a prince with a moral mission, the chosen one, the one destined (as he saw it) to move films up to better things. And he is combating a mercenary and reactionary crowd.

In order to get to the top of his profession and to achieve what he believes is his *mission* and destiny, a young man seizes power, uses it ruthlessly, and in the process cuts himself off, loses his humanity. Then he, through the loss of his wife and the following loneliness, through the passing of time, through a monastic life, realizes what has happened to him. The main thing that makes him realize that is an encounter with his feminine ideal of beauty, romance and goodness. Having realized how dried up and toughened and serene he has become, he reaches back to regain his humanity. When he does this he exposes what he has never exposed before, his vulnerability. His naked neck. When he exposes this, he is killed.

STAHR'S MISSION

THEME

MY WORK
IN THE THEATRE
AND WITH ACTORS

KAZAN AS ACTOR

IN THE THEATRE

Overleaf: Elia Kazan and Kirk Douglas on the set of *The Arrangement* (1969).
Below: Elia Kazan (*first row, fourth from left*) in *Johnny Johnson* (1936) by Paul Green.
Right: Elia Kazan (a make-up session at the Group Theatre).

Elia Kazan in *Paradise Lost* (1935) by Clifford Odets.

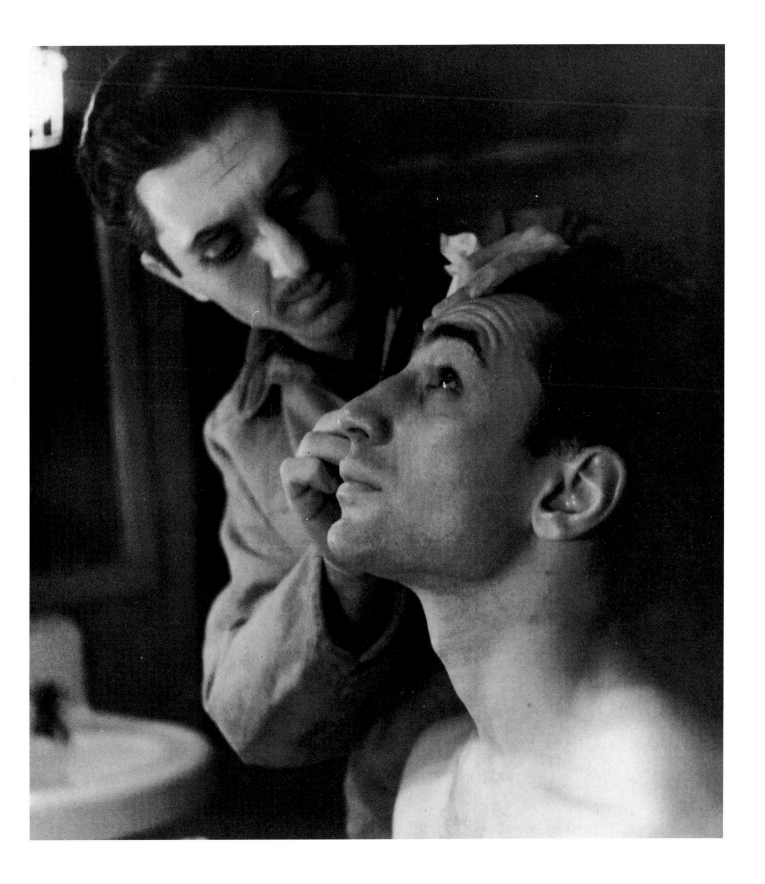

Elia Kazan and Roman Bohnens in *Golden Boy* (1937) by Clifford Odets.

Curt Conway, Lee J. Cobb, Roman Bohnens, Grover Burgess, Elia Kazan and Louis Polan in *Golden Boy* (1937) by Clifford Odets.

Elia Kazan and Frances
Farmer in *Golden Boy*
(1937) by Clifford Odets.

Art Smith, Maurice
Carnovsky, Jane Wyatt,
Elia Kazan and Will Lee in
Night Music (1940) by
Clifford Odets.

Elia Kazan and Burgess
Meredith in *Liliom* (1940)
by Ferenc Molnar.

I was an actor for eight years. My last part was in *Five Alarm Waltz*; it was inspired by the American writer William Saroyan, a great talent, so pretty eccentric, but no more than I can be when I get going. I decided to play one scene wearing only the bottom half of my underwear, for which I was mocked by the most important New York drama critic of the day, Brooks Atkinson. He wrote a teasing paragraph about me which I took as derogatory and insulting. I decided never again to give a critic the opportunity of making fun of me. And I stood by that decision.

The few successes I managed to have as an actor were in "tough guy" and gangster parts. This is ironic – because I'm a gentle, rather timid man who, when possible, avoids physical confrontation. But they told me that I was very menacing in *Golden Boy*. I don't know how that could have happened.

Elia Kazan and Louise Platt in *Five Alarm Waltz* by Robert Lewis.

Elia Kazan (*right*) in *Café Universal* (1934) by Ralph Steiner.

Elia Kazan in *Pie in the Sky* (1934) by Ralph Steiner.

Elia Kazan and James
Cagney in *City for
Conquest* (1940) by Anatol
Litvak.

Elia Kazan in *Blues in the
Night* (1941) by Anatol
Litvak.

Unpublished
notes, 1985.

THE PLAYS I DIRECTED

DIMITROFF

Dimitroff was an agit-prop play, intended for our equivalent of the "blue shirts". It was intended for believers; it served to lead cheers. I can't believe it successfully influenced anyone in favor of its Communist hero. I was a Communist at the time and doing what was expected of me. The play receives attention now only from those archivists for whom everything is, in one sense, equally important. This work, however, has no importance – except as a footnote, a small one, for my history. The hero was played by a fine actor, J. Edward Bromberg, a Communist with me in the Group Theatre's cell; he was to be black-listed and would die alone in a London rooming house.

Casey Jones was written by a man who was not to achieve any fame as a playwright but a good deal as an author; Robert Ardrey wrote *African Genesis* and several other books about the origin of man. He was from the Midwest and was a man who esteemed the solitary, "stand-up" hero who was fast fading from the American scene. It was a rather feeble play with a basically senti-mental premiss. It was, however, notable for its setting, a locomotive which seemed to move on stage. This was by a designer who never achieved the recognition he should have, Mordecai Gorelik. An early espouser of Bertolt Brecht, his own work was spare realism, not "epic" in any of that much misused word's meanings. I learned a valuable lesson from "Max" Gorelik: a play should take place not BEFORE a set-ting but INSIDE a setting. He meant by this that a stage setting should be an environ-ment not a backdrop.

CASEY JONES

THE YOUNG GO
FIRST

The Young Go First is a play I did when I was a Communist and it protests the social situation and specifically the situation in the Civilian Conservation Corps, one of the "alphabet soup" social services that were set up in the New Deal by Franklin Roose-velt. It was played by a theatre group, of which I was a member when I was a Com-munist, called the Theatre of Action. A member of the cast was Nicholas Ray, who became a famous film director twenty years later. Another member of the The-atre of Action was Martin Ritt, who also won a great deal of fame and respect later as a director of film features. The most interesting memory I have of the produc-tion was that when we discovered we had no third act, I gave the actors "beats" of action to improvise on, had a stenographer in the front row taking down what the actors said, had those notes typed and made a third act from what I had. It worked too. Those were the days!

Thunder Rock was the other play by Ardrey that the Theatre of Action did and I directed. It was a reflective, discursive play, and whereas it failed in the United States, it was a success in England, where the leading role was performed by Michael Redgrave. Again it featured in its central role a figure out of American folk imagin-ing: a lighthouse keeper who retired to this profession so he could reflect on the sad state of the world and play scenes with people out of the past whom he'd bring to life by his lively imagination. It also con-tained a yearning for a fast disappearing, purer, sturdier, more individualistic America.

THUNDER ROCK

Opposite: Elia Kazan and
Arthur Miller on the set of
Death of a Salesman
(1949).

It's Up to You. During the Second World War, I worked for our Department of Agri-culture. One of their problems was to make

IT'S UP TO YOU

Charles Bickford (*right*) in *Casey Jones* (1938) by Robert Ardrey.

the American public aware of the importance of rationing – sympathetic to its necessity. My task was to cook up a play-performance in the style of the so-called *Living Newspaper* about rationing. So I did. We had some novelties there, such as a woman on stage having a dialogue scene with her image, projected on a motion-picture screen of great size behind her. Another was casting the fine "revolutionary dancer", Helen Tamiris, as a steak. She did it very well. I enjoyed myself.

CAFÉ CROWN

Café Crown was a charming play by a very minor playwright, a nostalgic look at a restaurant which served as hangout for the actors of the Jewish theatre. I liked the play, but it was too mild for the Broadway traffic. It was all atmosphere and Jewish theatre jokes.

The Skin of Our Teeth made my reputation as a Broadway director. It was the work of Thornton Wilder, a man influenced by Joyce but quite unlike him. It was a rather bookish jape and provided excellent roles for four theatre stars, Freddie March, Tallulah Bankhead, Florence March and Florence Reed; it was my business to keep them in order. I didn't really direct the production, only the actors. The set was designed without my concurrence by the producer, Michael Myerberg, and wasn't what the author wanted. The play was timely, coming when the United States had just entered the war and everyone was

THE SKIN OF OUR TEETH

160

Frances Farmer, Lee J. Cobb, Luther Adler and Morris Carnovsky in *Thunder Rock* (1939) by Robert Ardrey.

concerned about the race surviving. It did – at least that war – and so did the play, which was an enormous success. I'm not sure how much I contributed to this, but to be "associated" – that's the word – with a success makes a reputation in our theatre. This play is revived again and again and is perfect for community theatres, college theatres and the like since it glides skilfully and engagingly over the issues and makes the viewer feel he has culture.

ONE TOUCH OF VENUS

One Touch of Venus. I had three tries at the musical theatre form and I'm not proud of my work in any of the three. *One Touch of Venus* was a great success, but mostly if

not altogether because of the work and presence of Mary Martin, Agnes deMille and the dancer, Sono Osato. These women were remarkable talents. I learned a great lesson from the *corps de ballet* in the production, watching how hard they worked, how disciplined they were. Actors now don't work nearly as hard nor are they as ambitious artistically – I don't mean in their careers but in their artistic potential and capabilities. I believe Miss deMille, whose dances were brilliant, was the most dominating personality I ever worked with, so dominating in fact that I was reduced to a kind of stage manager who watched her work in amazement and arranged the lights and stage space to her bidding. I soon became weary of this kind of subservient role, and after my next musical I decided to admit that this was not my best field.

JACOBOWSKY AND THE COLONEL

Jacobowsky and the Colonel – a play written originally by Franz Werfel, adapted (whatever that means) for the theatre by Clifford Odets and then rewritten with humor and a skilful human touch by S. N. Behrman. The production was quite good and it was inhabited by a genius, Oscar Karlweiss. He was at his best in this production, he had a deftness and a charm which does not presently exist in our theatre. He played the role of a Jew, Jacobowsky, fleeing south in France before the advancing Nazis. His companion in the ride to freedom is a Polish Colonel who shares many of the less attractive qualities of the Nazis. How Jacobowsky – that is Karlweiss, for the two soon become synonymous – tantalizes, and slips away from the Nazis and his more immediate tormentor, the Polish Colonel, is the body of the play. The direction had its merits too.

DEEP ARE THE ROOTS

Deep are the Roots is the first play I did when I came back from the war and is a play – now completely old-fashioned – of social protest. The set-up, a black coming to self-awareness in an environment of the deep South, is now of no interest. We've gone past its message and its drama. The leading role was well played by an actress with a luminous quality, Barbara Bel Geddes, and all that I remember from the play is her face at certain moments. It was, I believe, the high point of her professional life and she was never to surpass it.

ALL MY SONS

All My Sons was Arthur Miller's first success. It was a well-constructed play in the Ibsen tradition. A son finds the corruption in his father. I did it well, cast it well and it affected the audience of the time, who were seriously concerned about war profiteering and so on, the loosening of morals in the society. It was a strong and unequivocal play, which made its point clearly and unmistakably. Well played by a group of

Helen Tamiris in *It's Up to You* (1941), a mixture of theatre, cinema and dance.

actors who became known very soon as part of my "stock company", it had the earmarks of the kind of production for which I'd become famous. The playwright whom it most influenced was Tennessee Williams, who thought it eloquent.

TRUCKLINE CAFÉ

Truckline Café is a work by Maxwell Anderson, who was an outstanding playwright of his day, although he is now forgotten. The play is forgotten too, even by me. Except for this. It had a five-minute scene with a young man who completely dominated the stage and the audience with an overwhelming emotional power that is now in my memory and then on stage unforgettable. The young man's name was MARLON BRANDO. His performance here is why I knew enough to cast him in *Streetcar Named Desire*.

A STREETCAR NAMED DESIRE

A Streetcar Named Desire. This famous play deserves its reputation. It is perfectly constructed and eloquently written and it's from the heart, Williams's heart. It was beautifully played by an excellent cast who gave it a "company" feeling. Jessica Tandy, Marlon Brando, Kim Hunter, Karl Malden, all outdid themselves and I doubt if the play could be done better – more flashily perhaps but not more truly or soundly. The performance had the benefit of a landmark setting by Jo Mielziner, one that would be imitated in years to come by many designers, a setting on the shadowy border between fantasy and realism. This is the strongest play by this author because it dramatizes one of his central concerns, the crushing of the tender and spiritual values by the more animalistic sides of our society. The interesting thing is that the author – for he is Blanche – is attracted by the hardier antagonist who will in the end crush and destroy him. In the deepest sense, this is a personal play, even autobiographical. It's a poet revealing his soul.

DEATH OF A SALESMAN

Death of a Salesman is my favorite play partly because it touches on my relationship with my father. It is the only play I directed at which men in the audience, men of advanced years, cried. I did this play well inside a magnificent setting by Jo Mielziner. It had a landmark performance, one that will not be matched, by Lee J. Cobb. The central figure whom he played, Willy Loman, has become a symbolic figure in American culture. The sweep of the play is so powerful that it carries the audience past some defects – they don't matter. It plays on every father's hope that he can help his son, that his son will love him and value him, that he will prove his own worth through the achievements of his son. And equally, it conveys the terrible pain which comes from a father's disappointment in his son, who hasn't lived up to his hopes. This play has what all classics have, a resonance beyond any particular lines or scenes, a core of feeling that is unforgettable.

Morris Carnovsky (*centre*) in *Café Crown* (1942) by Hy S. Kraft.

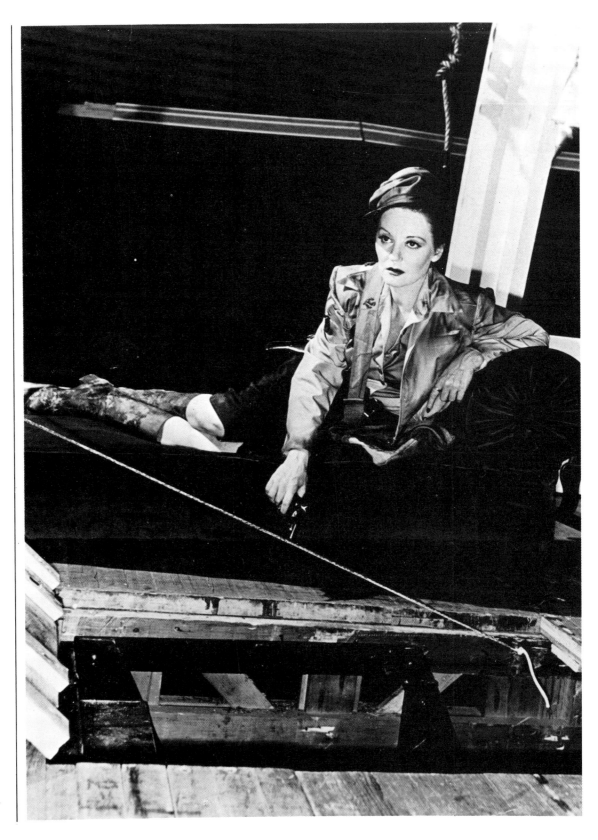

Tallulah Bankhead in *The Skin of our Teeth* (1942) by Thornton Wilder.

CAMINO REAL

Camino Real is a play which I enjoyed doing because I constantly felt that my capabilities and technique were being stretched. It contained music and dancing and had a décor, especially in the costumes, that suggested the work of the Mexican primitive artist, Posada. I did the play with a cast entirely from the Actors' Studio and it had a wonderful feeling of ensemble play. Unfortunately the play had poetry and imagination but no cumulative dramatic drive. It had brilliant scenes but not a crescendo of tension which would come from one scene leading into another into another and so on. In effect it had no third act and died, as the poem goes, with "a whimper". I feel that hidden in the folds of its fabric was an element of self-pity, an emotion that appears now and then in Williams's work but not in his best plays.

TEA AND SYMPATHY

Tea and Sympathy is a perfect play, small, modest, tender, sensitive, and beautifully constructed. These plays, the fruit of the first intense experience of a lifetime – *Glass Menagerie* of Tennessee Williams is another, *Awake and Sing*, still another – pop up as if by some divine accident. All I had to do was not make bad mistakes – such as over-dramatizing, over-theatricalizing the play. And to provide it with the correct setting in the scale and size suited to a play of modest intimate action. And, above all perhaps, cast it right. Robert Anderson provided us with the right actress for the role in Deborah Kerr, who gave a performance of sympathetic sensitivity equal to the best features and scenes of the play. From first to last, the experience was the simplest, the quickest and the easiest I had in the theatre and it left me wondering: why can't every play be as easy to produce? I've done two other perfectly constructed plays but of a much grander scale, *Streetcar Named Desire* and *Death of a Salesman*. Anderson's play is that of a miniaturist and he doesn't make one false step.

Left: Elia Kazan surrounded by his actors on the set of *Jacobowsky and the Colonel* (1944) by Franz Werfel. *Left to right:* Oscar Karlweiss, Louis Calhern, Annabella and J. Edward Bromberg. *Top right:* Annabella and Louis Calhern in *Jacobowsky and the Colonel* (1944) by Franz Werfel.

CAT ON A HOT TIN ROOF

Cat on a Hot Tin Roof is Williams's favorite play of his own – so he says. It has the most brilliant speech, which amounts to the entire second act, and this speech was brilliantly rendered by Burl Ives, a "folk singer" who had never performed in the professional theatre before. The difference Williams and I had about the third act caused quite a stir in the annals of our theatre, emphasized by the publication of the text when the author published both the third act he preferred – one we didn't use – and the one I preferred, which we did use. The author forgot that I offered twice to restore his original third act – if he wished. But apparently he preferred the one he characterized as more "commercial". The play was a great success and again was well played by a comparatively unknown cast – not by great stars. A feature I liked was the setting which was, this time, totally unrealistic, a platform of a triangular shape which protruded into the audience. From its point, Ives stood to deliver the great second act speech.

DARK AT THE TOP OF THE STAIRS

Dark at the Top of the Stairs is a childhood memory play by William Inge. This is a sensitively written play in a minor key, a play of deceptive depth. The first impression it makes is not distinguished – it seems like the kind of story featured in women's magazines, those intended to pass the time

Lee J. Cobb and Howard Smith in *Death of a Salesman* (1949) by Arthur Miller.

Mildred Dunnock and Arthur Kennedy in *Death of a Salesman* (1949) by Arthur Miller.

for housewives. But slowly it gets deeper and more poignant until we can't help feeling, as we sit before it, that the author has tapped a vein of the most genuine emotion. Again it was played by actors not of star calibre but perfect for their roles. This had become my trademark. The value of the evening did not rest on a supercharged performer. It was, in all, a quiet and most affecting night in the theatre – but it is rarely revived now because that kind of offering has been overwhelmed by what's on TV.

JB

JB is a play that won the Pulitzer Prize and received all kinds of kudos but which I found terribly dull. Then why did I do it? Because it gave an opportunity to do a kind of production that I had not done before, one in which there is bold, unrealistic picturization and the kind of acting that amounts to choreographed movement. I directed the play as I might have a ballet and there is nothing realistic about it. I think the theme – that of the long-suffering Job as a contemporary businessman, reached its audience and affected them. But I didn't respond to the poetry. The fact is that I have little ear for poetry and little patience for it in the theatre unless it's Shakespeare's – and not all of his. The outstanding thing about the show was the superb setting by the other designer whom I esteemed equally with Mielziner, Boris Aronson.

SWEET BIRD OF YOUTH

Sweet Bird of Youth is the last play of Williams's that I did and it is imperfectly constructed – there seem to be two stories here, alternating, and the one that the author should have developed into the main story line is not particularly well developed and written, while what amounts to the subsidiary story is beautifully written and memorable. This play offered a remarkable performance by the actress Geraldine Page, and a good one by Paul Newman, which made me feel he should work on the stage more. I did one of my "naughty" tricks here. Feeling the second act, the one without Miss Page was weak, I had a

great TV screen erected and while Boss Ginley, the southern bigot, made his speech, his image is projected directly behind him as he speaks. The effect is certainly startling but it makes any simply human intercourse that might follow seem ordinary and perhaps dull.

After the Fall was the first Lincoln Center Repertory Theatre production that I did and the only one which was worth a damn. We mounted it in a temporary theatre on the campus of New York University downtown. We carved out an amphitheatre shape, poured concrete in and covered it with a pre-fabricated steel roof, and it was a striking theatre occasion. I found the first act very dull. There was a character there whom Miller identified with me in relation to my testimony; he was not unsympathetically portrayed – nor was he sympathetically portrayed. The leading figure, Quentin, who could pass for Miller, I suppose, talked to the audience endlessly and I thought without much interest. Then came the second act and on stage came the character based on Marilyn Monroe, Miller's second wife, played brilliantly by Barbara Loden. Miller here was amazingly honest; he put in the mouth of this character all the anger that Marilyn had against him at the end. Miss Loden played the gamut of emotions from the naïve, but manipulative young flirt to the drug-obsessed, fading woman with murderous feelings.

AFTER THE FALL

The Changeling is a play of Elizabethan England and I thought it a good play, a strong play. But my production was miserable, it didn't work at all. It discouraged me, once and for all, from doing anything with the so-called classical theatre. I decided after my experience with this production that I had no feeling or genuine interest for any but contemporary plays on contemporary subjects. I still believe this true. It's my failing.

THE CHANGELING

The Chain. I finally tried to write a play in 1984. It taught me to value playwrights. I failed.

THE CHAIN

Elia Kazan directing Vivien
Leigh and Kim Hunter in
the film version of *A
Streetcar Named Desire*
(1950).

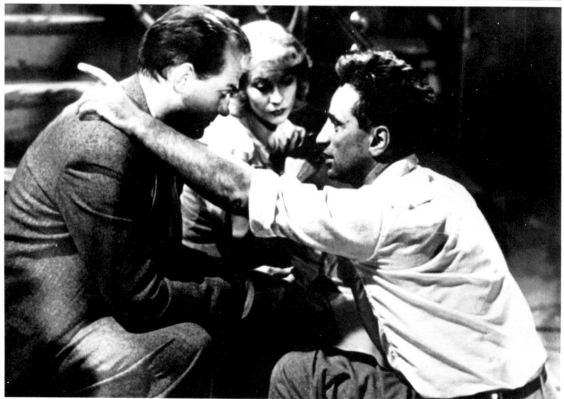

Elia Kazan directing Karl
Malden and Vivien Leigh
in the film version of *A
Streetcar Named Desire*
(1950).

NOTEBOOK FOR "A STREETCAR NAMED DESIRE"

A thought – directing finally consists of turning psychology into behavior.

Theme – this is a message from the dark interior. This little twisted, pathetic, confused bit of light and culture puts out a cry. It is snuffed out by the crude forces of violence, insensibility and vulgarity which exist in our South – and this cry is the play.

Style – one reason a "style", a stylized production, is necessary is that a subjective factor – Blanche's memories, inner life, emotions – are a real factor. We cannot really understand her behavior unless we see the effect of her present behavior.

This play is a poetic tragedy. We are shown the final dissolution of a person of worth, who once had great potential, and who, even as she goes down, has worth exceeding that of the "healthy", coarse-grained figures who kill her.

Blanche is a social type, an emblem of a dying civilization, making its last curlicued and romantic exit. All her behavior patterns are those of the dying civilization she represents. In other words her behavior is *social*. Therefore find social modes! This is the source of the play's stylization and the production's style and color. Likewise Stanley's behavior is *social* too. It is the basic animal cynicism of today. "Get what's coming to you! Don't waste a day! Eat, drink, get yours!" This is the basis of his stylization, of the choice of his props. All props should be stylized: they should have a color, shape and weight that spell: style.

An effort to put poetic names on scenes to edge me into stylizations and physicalizations. Try to keep each scene in terms of Blanche.

1 Blanche comes to the last stop at the end of the line.

2 Blanche tries to make a place for herself.

3 Blanche breaks them apart, but when they come together, Blanche is more alone than ever!

4 Blanche, more desperate because more excluded, tries the direct attack and makes the enemy who will finish her.

5 Blanche finds that she is being tracked down for the kill. She must work fast.

6 Blanche suddenly finds, suddenly makes for herself, the only possible, perfect man for her.

7 Blanche comes out of the happy bathroom to find that her own doom has caught up with her.

8 Blanche fights her last fight. Breaks down. Even Stella deserts her.

Elia Kazan in the dressing room of Jessica Tandy, who played the part of Blanche on stage in *A Streetcar Named Desire* (1947) by Tennessee Williams.

9 Blanche's last desperate effort to save herself by telling the whole truth. The *truth dooms her.*

10 Blanche escapes out of this world. She is brought back by Stanley and destroyed.

11 Blanche is disposed of.

The style – the real deep style – consists of one thing only: to find behavior that's truly social, significantly typical, at each moment. It's not so much what Blanche has done – it's how she does it – with such style, grace, manners, old-world trappings and effects, props, tricks, swirls, etc., that they seem anything but vulgar.

And for the other characters, too, you face the same problem. To find the Don Quixote character for them. *This is a poetic tragedy, not a realistic or naturalistic one. So you must find a Don Quixote scheme of things for each.*

Stylized acting and direction is to realistic acting and direction as poetry is to prose. The acting must be styled, not in the obvious sense. (Say nothing about it to the producer and actors.) But you will fail unless you find this kind of poetic realization for the behavior of these people.

BLANCHE

"Blanche is desperate."

"This is the End of the Line of the Streetcar Named Desire."

Spine – find protection: the tradition of the old South says that it must be through another person.

Her problem has to do with her tradition. Her notion of what a woman should be. She is stuck with this "ideal". It is her. It is her ego. Unless she lives by it, she cannot live; in fact her whole life has been for nothing. Even the Alan Gray incident, as she now tells it and believes it to have been, is a necessary piece of romanticism. Essentially, in outline, she tells what happened, but it also serves the demands of her

notion of herself, to make her *special* and different, out of the tradition of the romantic ladies of the past: Swinburne, Wm Morris, Pre-Raphaelites, etc. This way it serves as an excuse for a great deal of her behavior.

Because this image of herself cannot be accomplished in reality, certainly not in the South of our day and time, it is her effort and practice to *accomplish it in fantasy*. Everything that she does in *reality* too is colored by this necessity, this compulsion to be *special*. So, in fact, *reality becomes fantasy too.* She makes it so!

The variety essential to the play, and to Blanche's playing and to Jessica Tandy's achieving the role, demands that she be a "heavy" at the beginning. For instance: contemplate the inner character contradiction: bossy yet helpless, domineering yet shaky, etc. The audience at the beginning should see her bad effect on Stella, want Stanley to tell her off. He does. He exposes her and then gradually, as they see how genuinely in pain, how actually desperate she is, how warm, tender and loving she can be (the Mitch story), how freighted with need she is – then they begin to go with her. They begin to realize that they are sitting in at the death of something extraordinary . . . colorful, varied, passionate, lost, witty, imaginative, of her own integrity . . . and then they feel the tragedy. In the playing too there can be a growing sincerity and directness.

The thing about the "tradition" in the nineteenth century was that *it worked then.* It made a woman feel important, with her own secure positions and functions, her own special worth. It also made a woman at that time *one with her society.* But *today* the tradition is an anachronism which simply does not function. *It does not work.* So while Blanche must believe it because it makes her special, because it makes her sticking by Belle Reve an act of heroism, rather than an absurd romanticism, still *it does not work.* It makes Blanche feel *alone, outside of her society.* Left out, insecure,

Vivien Leigh and Kim
Hunter in *A Streetcar
Named Desire* (1950).

shaky. The airs the "tradition" demands isolate her further, and every once in a while, her resistance weakened by drink, she breaks down and seeks human warmth and contact where she can find it, not on her terms, on theirs; the merchant, the travelling salesman and the others ... among whom the vulgar adolescent soldiers seem the most innocent. Since she cannot integrate these episodes, she rejects them, begins to forget them, begins to live in fantasy, begins to rationalize and explain them to herself thus: "I

never was hard or self-sufficient enough ... men don't see women unless they are in bed with them. They don't admit their existence except when they're love-making. You've got to have your existence admitted by someone if you are going to receive someone's protection," etc. As if you had to apologize for needing human contact! Also n.b. above – the word: protection. That is what she, as a woman in the tradition, so desperately needs. That's what she comes to Stella for, Stella and her husband. Not finding it from them she tries

Jessica Tandy in the stage part of Blanche in *A Streetcar Named Desire* (1947).

372-36

Vivien Leigh in the film role of Blanche in *A Streetcar Named Desire* (1950).

to get it from Mitch. *Protection*. A haven, a *harbor*. She is a refugee, punch drunk, and on the ropes, making her last stand, trying to keep up a gallant front, because she is a proud person. But really if Stella doesn't provide her haven, *where is she to go?* She's a misfit, a liar, her "airs" alienate people, she must act superior to them which alienates them further. She doesn't know how to work. So she can't make a living. She's really helpless. She needs someone to help her. Protection. She's a last dying relic of the last century now adrift in our unfriendly day. From time to time, for reasons of simple human loneliness and need, she goes to pieces, smashes her tradition ... then goes back to it. This conflict has developed into a terrible crisis. All she wants is a haven: "I want to rest! I want to breathe quietly again ... just think! If it happens! I can leave here and have a home of my own ... "

If this is a romantic tragedy, what is its inevitability and what is the tragic flaw? In the Aristotelian sense, the flaw is the need to be superior, special (or *her* need for protection and what it means to her), the "tradition". This creates an apartness so intense, a loneliness so gnawing that only a complete breakdown, a refusal, as it were, to contemplate what she's doing, a *binge* as it were, a destruction of all her standards, a desperate violent ride on the Streetcar Named Desire can break through the walls of her tradition. The tragic flaw creates the circumstances, inevitably, that destroy her. More later.

Try to find an entirely different character, a self-dramatized and self-romanticized character for Blanche to play in each scene. She is playing 11 different people. This will give it a kind of changeable and shimmering surface it should have. And all these 11 self-dramatized and romantic characters should be out of the romantic tradition of the Pre-Bellum South, etc. Example: Sc. 2 Gay Miss Devil-may-care.

There is another, simpler and equally terrible contradiction in her own nature. She won't face her physical or sensual side. She calls it "brutal desire". She thinks she sins when she gives in to it ... yet she does give in to it, out of loneliness ... but by calling it "brutal desire", she is able to separate it from her "real self", her "cultured", refined self. Her tradition makes no allowance, allows no space for this very real part of herself. So she is constantly in conflict, not at ease, sinning. *She's still looking for something that doesn't exist today, a gentleman,* who will treat her like a virgin, marry her, protect her, defend and maintain her honor, etc. She wants an old-fashioned wedding dressed in white ... and still she does things out of "brutal desire" that make this impossible. *All this too is tradition.*

She has worth too – she is better than Stella. She says: "There has been some kind of progress ... Such things as art – as poetry and music – such kinds of new light have come into the world ... in some kinds of people some kinds of tenderer feelings have had some little beginning that we've got to make *grow*! And cling to, and hold as our flag! In this dark march toward whatever it is we're approaching ... don't ... don't hang back with the brutes!" And though the direct psychological motivation for this is jealousy and personal frustration, still she, alone and abandoned in the crude society of New Orleans back streets, is the *only voice of light*. It is flickering and, in the course of the play, goes out. But it is valuable because it is unique.

Blanche is a butterfly in a jungle looking for just a little momentary protection, doomed to a sudden, early violent death. The more I work on Blanche, incidentally, the less insane she seems. She is caught in a fatal inner contradiction, but in another society, she *would* work. In Stanley's society, no!

This is like a classic tragedy. Blanche is Medea or someone pursued by the Harpies, the Harpies being *her own nature*. Her inner sickness pursues her like *doom* and makes it impossible for her to attain the one thing she needs, the only thing she needs: a safe harbor.

An effort to phrase Blanche's spine: to find *protection*, to find something to hold onto, some strength in whose protection she can live, like a sucker shark or a parasite. The tradition of *woman* (or all women) can only live through the strength of someone else. Blanche is entirely dependent. Finally the doctor!

Blanche is an outdated creature, approaching extinction . . . like the dinosaur. She is about to be pushed off the edge of the earth. On the other hand she is a heightened version, an artistic intensification of all women. That is what makes the play universal. Blanche's special relation to all women is that she is at that critical point where *the one thing above all else that she is dependent on – her attraction for men – is beginning to go.* Blanche is like all women, dependent on a man, looking for one to hang onto: only *more so!*

So beyond being deeply desperate, Blanche is in a hurry. She'll be pushed off the earth soon. She carries her doom in her character. Also, her past is chasing her, catching up with her. Is it any wonder that she tries to attract each and every man she meets? She'll even take that protected feeling, that needed feeling, that superior feeling, for a moment. Because, at least for a moment, that anxiety, the hurt and the pain will be quenched. The sex act is the opposite of loneliness. Desire is the opposite of death. For a moment the anxiety is still, for a moment the complete desire and concentration of a man is on her. He clings to you. He may say I love you. All else is anxiety, loneliness and being adrift.

Compelled by her nature (she must be special, superior) she makes it impossible with Stanley and Stella. She acts in a way that succeeds in being destructive. But the last bit of luck is with her. She finds the only man on earth whom she suits, a man who is looking for a dominant woman. For an instant she is happy. But her past catches up with her. Stanley, whom she's antagonized by her destructiveness aimed at his home, but especially by her need to be

superior, uses her past, which he digs up, to destroy her. Finally she takes refuge in fantasy. She must have protection, closeness, love, safe harbor. The only place she can obtain them any longer is in her own mind. She "goes crazy".

Blanche is a stylized character, she should be played, should be dressed, should move like a stylized figure. What is the physicalization of an aristocratic woman pregnant with her own doom? . . . Behaving by a tradition that dooms her in this civilization, in this "culture"? All her behavior patterns are *old-fashioned, pure tradition.* All as if jellied in rote –

Why does the "Blues" music fit the play? The Blues is an expression of the loneliness and rejection, the exclusion and isolation of the Negro and their (opposite) longing for love and connection. Blanche too is "looking for a home", abandoned, friendless. "I don't know where I'm going, but I'm going." Thus the Blues piano catches the soul of Blanche, the miserable unusual human side of the girl which is beneath her frenetic duplicity, her trickery, lies, etc. It tells, it emotionally reminds you what all the fireworks are caused by.

Blanche – physically. Must at all times give a single impression: her social mask is: *the High-Bred Genteel Lady in Distress.* Her past, her destiny, her falling from grace is just a surprise . . . then a tragic contradiction. But the mask never breaks down.

The only way to understand any character is through yourself. Everyone is much more alike than they willingly admit. Even as frantic and fantastic a creature as Blanche is created by things you have felt and known, *if you'll dig for them and be honest about what you see.*

Spine – hold onto Stanley (Blanche the antagonist).

One reason Stella submits to Stanley's solution at the end, is perfectly ready to, is that she has an unconscious hostility towards Blanche. Blanche is so patronizing, demanding and superior towards her ... makes her so useless, old-fashioned and helpless ... everything that Stanley has got her out of. Stanley has made a woman out of her. Blanche immediately returns her to the subjugation of childhood, younger-sister-ness.

Stella would have been Blanche except for Stanley. She now knows what, how much Stanley means to her health. So ... no matter what Stanley does ... she must cling to him, as she does to life itself. To return to Blanche would be to return to the subjugation of the tradition.

The play is a triangle. Stella is the apex. Unconsciously, Stella wants Blanche to go to Mitch because that will take Blanche off Stella.

And there is a terrific conflict between Blanche and Stella, especially in Stella's feelings. Blanche in effect in Sc. 1 *resubjugates* Stella. Stella loves her, hates her, fears her, pities her, is really through with her. Finally rejects her for Stanley.

All this of course Stella is aware of only unconsciously. It becomes a matter of conscious choice only in Sc. 11 ... the climax of the play as it is the climax of the triangle story.

Stella is a refined girl who has found a kind of salvation or realization, *but at a terrific price.* She keeps her eyes closed, even stays in bed as much as possible so that she won't realize, won't *feel* the pain of this terrific price. She walks around as if narcotized, as if sleepy, as if in a daze. She is waiting for night. She's waiting for the dark where Stanley makes her feel *only him* and she has no reminder of the price she is paying. She wants no intrusion from the other world. She is drugged, trapped. She's in a sensual stupor. She shuts out all challenge all day long. She loafs, does her hair, her nails, fixes a dress, doesn't eat much, but prepares Stanley's dinner and waits for Stanley. She hopes for no other meaning from life. Her pregnancy just makes it more so. Stanley is in her day and night. Her entire attention is to make herself pretty and attractive for Stanley, kill time till night. In a way she is actually narcotized all day. She is buried alive in her flesh. She's half asleep. She is glazed across her eyes. She doesn't seem to see much. She laughs incessantly like a child tickled and stops abruptly as the stimuli, the tickling, stops and returns to the same condition, a pleasantly drugged child. Give her all kinds of narcotized business.

She has a paradise – a serenely limited paradise when Blanche enters – but Blanche makes her consider Stanley, judge Stanley and find him wanting, for the first time. But it is too late. In the end she returns to Stanley.

Stella is doomed too. She has sold herself out for a temporary solution. She's given up all hope, everything, just to live for Stanley's pleasures. So she is dependent on Stanley's least whim. But this can last only as long as Stanley wants her. And *secondly* and *chiefly* – Stella herself cannot live narcotized forever. There is more to her. She begins to feel, even in the sex act, *taken,* unfulfilled – not recognized ... and besides, she's deeper, needs more variety. Her only hope is her children and, like so many women, she will begin to live more and more for her children.

She tries to conceal from herself her true needs through hiding and drugging herself in a sex relationship. But her real needs, for tenderness, for the several aspects of living, for realization in terms of herself – not only in terms of Stanley – *still live ... she can't kill them* by ignoring them. Blanche, despite apparent failure, makes her realize certain things about Stanley. She hugs Stanley in Sc. 4 out of despera-

Marlon Brando and Kim Hunter in *A Streetcar Named Desire* (1950).

178

tion, and out of a need to silence her doubts by the violence of sexual love (the "old reliable") . . . but Blanche has succeeded in calling Stella's attention to her own "sell-out" . . . she never sees Stanley the same way again.

Stella, at the beginning of the play, won't face a *hostility* (concealed from herself and unrecognized) towards Stanley. She is *so* dependent on him, so compulsively compliant. She is giving up so much of herself, quieting so many voices of protest. She is Stanley's slave. She has sold out most of her life. Latent in Stella is rebellion. Blanche arouses it.

Stella is plain out of her head about Stanley. She has to keep herself from constantly touching him. She can hardly keep her hands off him. She is setting little traps all the time to conquer his act of indifference (he talks differently at night, in bed). She embarrasses him (though he is secretly proud) by following him places. They have a game where he tries to shake her all the time and she pursues him, etc. He makes her a panther in bed. He is her first man, really; he made her a woman. He fulfilled her more than she knew possible and she has to stop herself from *crawling* after him. She's utterly *blind* as to what's wrong with Stanley. She's blind to it and she doesn't care, *until* Blanche arrives. At the end of the play, her life is entirely different. It will never be the same with Stanley again.

Note from Tennessee Williams on the fourth day of rehearsal: "Gadge – I am a bit concerned over Stella in Scene One. It seems to me that she has too much vivacity, at times she is bouncing around in a way that suggests a co-ed on a benzedrine kick. I know it is impossible to be literal about the description 'narcotized tranquillity' but I do think there is an important value in suggesting it, in contrast to Blanche's rather feverish excitability. Blanche is the quick, light one. Stella is relatively slow and almost indolent. Blanche mentions her 'Chinese philosophy' – the way she sits with her little hands folded like a cherub in a choir, etc. I think her natural passivity is one of the things that makes her acceptance of Stanley acceptable. She naturally 'gives in', accepts, lets things slide, she does not make much of an effort."

Spine – keep things his way (Blanche the antagonist).

The hedonist, objects, props, etc. Sucks on a cigar all day because he can't suck a teat. Fruit, food, etc. He's got it all figured out, what fits, what doesn't. The pleasure scheme. He has all the confidence of resurgent flesh.

Also with a kind of naïveté . . . even slowness . . . he means no harm. He wants to knock no one down. He only doesn't want to be taken advantage of. His code is simple-minded. He is adjusted *now* . . . later, as his sexual powers die, so will he; the trouble will come later, the "problems".

But what is the chink in his armor now, the contradiction? Why does Blanche get so completely under his skin? Why does he want to bring Blanche and, before her, Stella *down to his level*? It's as if he said: "I know I haven't got much, but no one has more and so no one's going to have more." It's the hoodlum aristocrat. He's deeply dissatisfied, deeply hopeless, deeply cynical . . . the physical immediate pleasures, if they come in a steady enough stream, quiet this *as long as no one gets more* . . . then his bitterness comes forth and he tears down the pretender. But Blanche he can't seem to do anything with. She can't come down to his level so he levels her with his sex. He brings her right down to his level, beneath him.

One of the important things for Stanley is that Blanche *would wreck his home.* Blanche is dangerous. She's destructive. She would soon have him and Stella fighting. He's got things the way he wants them around there and he does *not* want them upset by a phony, corrupt, sick, destruc-

STANLEY

180

Kim Hunter, Vivien Leigh and Marlon Brando in *A Streetcar Named Desire* (1950).

tive woman. *This makes Stanley right!* Are we going into the era of Stanley? He may be practical and right ... but what the hell does it leave us? Make this a removed objective characterization for Marlon Brando.

Choose Marlon's objects ... the things he loves and prizes: all sensuous and sensual – the shirt, the cigar, the beer (how it's poured and nursed, etc.).

The one thing that Stanley can't bear is someone who thinks that he or she is better than him. His only way of explaining himself – he thinks he stinks – is that everyone else stinks. This is symbolic. True of our National State of Cynicism. No values. There is nothing to command his loyalty. Stanley rapes Blanche because he has tried and tried to keep her down to his level. This way is the last. For a moment he succeeds. And then, in Scene 11, he has failed!

Stanley has got things his way. He fits into his environment. The culture and the civilization, even the neighborhood, etc., etc., the food, the drink, etc., are all his way. And he's got a great girl, with just enough

Overleaf: Karl Malden and Jessica Tandy on stage in *A Streetcar Named Desire* (1947).

Vivien Leigh and Karl Malden in *A Streetcar Named Desire* (1950).

hidden neuroticism for him – yet not enough to even threaten a real fight. Also their history is right: he conquered her. Their relationship is right: she waits up for him. Finally God and Nature gave him a fine sensory apparatus . . . he enjoys! The main thing the actor has to do in the early scenes is make the physical environment of Stanley, the *props* come to life.

Stanley is deeply indifferent. When he first meets Blanche he doesn't really seem to care if she strays or not. Stanley is interested in his own pleasures. He is completely self-absorbed to the point of fascination.

To physicalize this: he has a most annoying way of being preoccupied – or of busying himself with something else while people are talking with him, at him it becomes. Example, first couple of pages Scene 2. Stanley thinks Stella is very badly brought up. She can't do any of the ordinary things – he had a girl before this that could really cook, but she drank an awful lot. Also she, Stella, has a lot of airs, most of which he's knocked out of her by now, but which still crop up. Emphasize Stanley's love for Stella. It is rough, embarrassed and he rather truculently *won't show it*. But it is there. He's proud of her. When he's not on guard and looking at her his eyes suddenly shine. He is grateful, too, proud, satisfied. But he'd never show it, demonstrate it.

Stanley is supremely indifferent to everything except his own pleasure and comfort. He is marvelously selfish, a miracle of sensuous self-centredness. He builds a hedonist life, and fights to the death to defend it – but finally it is *not* enough to hold Stella

and

this philosophy is not successful even for him – because every once in a while the silenced, frustrated part of Stanley breaks loose in unexpected and unpredictable ways and we suddenly see, as in a burst of lightning, his real frustrated self. Usually his frustration is worked off by eating a lot, drinking a lot, gambling a lot, fornicating a lot. He's going to get very fat later. He's desperately trying to squeeze out happiness by living by *ball and jowl* . . . and it really doesn't work . . . because it simply stores up violence, until every *bar in the nation is full of Stanleys ready to explode*. He's desperately trying to drug his senses . . . overwhelming them with a constant round of sensation so that he will feel nothing else.

In Stanley sex goes under a disguise. Nothing is more erotic and arousing to him than "airs" . . . she thinks she's better than me . . . I'll show her . . . Sex equals domination . . . anything that challenges him – like calling him "common" – arouses him sexually.

In the case of Brando, the question of enjoyment is particularly important. Stanley feeds himself. His world is hedonist. But what does he enjoy? Sex equals sadism. It is his "equalizer". He conquers with his penis. But objects too – drunk. Conquest in poker, food . . . sweat. *Exercise*. But Enjoy! Not just cruel and *unpleasant* . . . but he never graduated from the baby who wants a constant nipple in his mouth. He yells when it's taken away.

As a character Stanley is most interesting in his "contradictions", his "soft" moments, his sudden pathetic little-tough-boy tenderness towards Stella. Scene 3 he cries like a baby. Somewhere in Scene 8 he almost makes it up with Blanche. In Scene 10 he *does* try to make it up with her – and except for her doing the one thing that most arouses him, both in anger and sex, he might have.

Elia Kazan with his actors
on the set of *A Streetcar
Named Desire* (1950).
Left to right: Karl Malden,
Kim Hunter, Marlon
Brando and Vivien Leigh.

MITCH

Spine – get away from his mother (Blanche the lever).

He wants the perfection his mother gave him . . . everything is approving, protective, *perfect for him*. Naturally no girl, today, no sensible, decent girl will give him this. But the tradition will.

Like Stella, Mitch hides from his own problem through mother-love.

Mitch is the end product of a matriarchy . . . his mother has robbed him of all daring, initiative, self-reliance. He does not face his own needs.

Mitch is Blanche's ideal in a comic form, 150 years late. He is big, tough, burly, has a rough southern voice and a manner of homespun, coarse, awkward, overgrown boy, with a heart of mush. He's like that character (who cries easy) in *Sing Out Sweet Land*. He is a little embarrassed by his strength in front of women. He is straight out of Mack Sennett comedy – but Malden has to create the reality of it, the truth behind that corny image. Against his blundering strength there is shown off the fragility and fragrance of a girl. Her delicacy. "Lennie" in *Mice and Men*.

Mitch, too, is most interesting in his basic contradictions. He doesn't want to be mother's boy. Goddamn it, he just can't help it. He does love his mother, but is a little embarrassed at how much. Blanche makes a man out of him, makes him important and grown-up. His mother – he dimly realizes – keeps him eternally adolescent, forever dependent.

Violence – he's full of sperm
                    energy
                    strength
the reason he's so clumsy with women is that he's so damn full of violent desire for them.

Mitch's Mask: He-man mama's boy. This mask is a traditional, "corny" one in American dramatic literature. But it is true.

This play contains the crucial struggle of Mitch's life. For Mitch instinctively and even consciously, to a degree, knows what's wrong with him. He is jibed at often enough. And in his guts he knows they're right. Mitch, in his guts, hates his mother. He loves her in a way – partially out of *early habit*, partially because she is clever – but much more fundamentally he *hates her*. It is a tragedy for him when he returns to her absolute sovereignty at the end. He will never meet another woman who will need him as much as Blanche and will need him to be a man as much as Blanche.

TENNESSEE WILLIAMS'S BICYCLE

Speech to the American Film Institute in homage to Tennessee Williams, November 1979.

There is something awkward about an occasion of this kind. The person honored generally sits with head bowed, shielding himself from the leaden posies about to be dropped on him. If he seems ill at ease, it's for good reason. These affairs are uncomfortably close to a memorial meeting, what is said too often a premature eulogy.

All of us who work in the arts dread the day when our talent dries up. We suspect that everyone will know we're done before we do. When old friends show signs of feeling sorry for us, we bridle. We reject compliments put in the past tense. Actually the better the artist the less likely he is to believe flattery of any kind. In his heart he knows better.

Two nights ago I had a disturbing dream, a dream of anxiety. It puzzled me: perhaps it will mean something to you.

I was on my way to this gathering, dressed as you see me. On a rather dark street corner, I came upon an unruly crowd. Shouts, cries, laughter, murmurs. Among the multitude was our guest of honor. He was dressed in a badly assembled assortment of clothes provided, I would say, by the Salvation Army. As I got closer, I saw that he was as he was when I first knew him thirty-odd years ago. He hadn't aged. I had. A nightmare.

"What are you doing here?" I demanded, self-righteously.

"What are you all dressed up for?" he came back. "You look like a waiter."

"I'm making a speech," I said.

"Making a speech! What in the world about?"

"About you, for chrissake. You're being honoured tonight. Have you forgotten?"

"How did they rope you into that?" He burst into laughter. His laugh in those days was a defiant cackle. "Well, see if you can find something good to say about me!" And he moved off.

"Where you going?" I shouted. "Go home and fix yourself up. You look terrible. Hurry. They're waiting for you."

"I'm busy tonight," he said.

He looked off. When I turned my head I saw a bike and its rider circusing through the crowd, front wheels pulled off the ground. "Give my regards to Gramercy Park," Tennessee said, "and farewell!"

"Tennessee," I protested, "there are some very distinguished people waiting for you and if you –"

I never finished the sentence. With a move that was acrobatic our guest of honor leaped upon the back of the bike which suddenly accommodated two in the space it had one. And they were off looking like nothing as much as a marlin standing on its tail in the Gulf Stream. Passing me they responded to my disapproval with the classic Italian gesture of scorn and rejection. Then they were gone leaving behind only the echo of that contrary cackling laugh.

I don't know what the dream means but I do have an idea where it comes from.

The first time I heard of this man was in 1935 when the directors of the Group Theatre, beguiled by the small flush of affluence which followed the production of the first Odets play, decided to give a prize annually to an emerging playwright. This worthy resolve lasted one year; the next season the Group was again broke. Fun while it lasted.

The single prize we gave that one season was to Bill Saroyan, who, I imagine, blew the money at a San Francisco crap table. The consensus of feeling of the rather erra-

Kim Hunter in *A Streetcar Named Desire* (1950).

186

tic trio who directed the affairs of the Group was for the Armenian from Fresno, but the play-reader of the organization, one Molly Thatcher[1], talked them into giving a second prize, one hundred dollars, to another young fellow whose ripened person is seated here at my right. He had not yet, as near as I remember, written a long play, but Molly was dead certain his one-acters showed a unique talent and that this talent must be encouraged.

But there was a problem. No one could find the man to give him the money. His agent, Audrey Wood, was consulted. "He's somewhere down there," she pointed in the general direction of the southern states of this union, "riding around on a bike."

I still think of him that way, not on a bicycle but sought for, appearing, disappearing, I never know quite where or why. Between our accidental meetings, I can't guess where to find him.

But I often think of him. And tonight I don't want to talk about his talent or his work – so much has been said about all that. I'll tell you a little of what he has meant to me as a person.

A friend of mine, Boris Aronson, the scene designer, a man who's seen a lot of traffic pass, is fond of saying: "Success is the problem. Not poverty. Success is more difficult to handle."

I suppose Boris takes for granted that poverty is tough – God knows he's been broke.

But studying his friends, and watching how they took the success which comes down like an avalanche in this culture, Boris concluded that it is success which destroys the man of talent more quickly and more surely than its opposite.

I'm not sure I agree. But, having watched those who have hit the quick jackpot from John Garfield to Warren Beatty, I know what Boris means.

[1]Elia Kazan's first wife.

187

What do they do, those sudden geniuses after the shower of gold?

If they are movie stars now, they may move to the top of Mulholland Drive overlooking the city of stars, there safely above the rest of humanity. They may put an electric fence around their homes, sleep in a large bed of eccentric shape, oval perhaps, and protect themselves from the common world with agents, lawyers, secretaries and attack dogs.

If the fortunate person is a playwright he suddenly begins to lecture here and there on any variety of subjects from playwriting to politics, his opinions increasingly absolute on all topics. He begins to listen to his old friends with a pontifical cock of his head, noting for himself and later likely for them what they are doing wrong.

If he's a novelist, he becomes a member of an international élite, a secret society of snobs as tightly bound as any in history, and with them spends his winters on the ski slopes of Switzerland. More than likely he will soon become president of the Writers' Guild of America.

If he's a director, he may provide himself with an estate in Connecticut or Hidden Valley, raise horses or Sealyhams and begin to put together a collection of art to match that of Sam Spiegel. He walks into Sardi's or the Bistro with his prestige over his shoulder like a magic cape to protect him from the knives of the world.

Well, what's wrong with all that? Nothing.

Except it has seemed to me that the wealth and status, the eminence and prestige serve to protect the artist from the burrs of fortune, the very experiences which gave birth to his talent.

With those springs stopped, he is in danger of drying up and often does. He can no longer be stung to life. His affluence protects him.

Somerset Maugham once said, "What has influenced my life more than anything else has been my stammer. Had I not stammered, I would probably have gone to Cambridge, perhaps become a don and every now and then published a dreary book about French literature."

But who is silly enough to go around looking for outrage and humiliation? Who courts discomfort?

You see it's a difficult problem.

Except for the few. They carry their trouble with them.

Our guest of honor over the years I've known him has certainly become socially more confident but I don't know if he really is. Look in the mirror of his work. Whatever he writes doesn't insist that you see things as he does. He lives in doubt. He knows that to ask a question is more important in art than to state a conclusion. Repeatedly while I was directing his plays, he'd say to me, "Let's have an area of mystery in that character, let's not try to explain everything."

Dostoevsky said the same thing of the Prince in *The Possessed*: "I want him to be everywhere mysterious."

Well, how do you keep yourself questing, how do you make sure that your very natural impulse to protect yourself does not protect you from the experiences that keep your talent alive?

I don't know. It certainly isn't anything you can arrange for yourself. It only happens involuntarily and because of what you are.

Look at the trivia. They tell a lot. Start from the outside.

Consider his costume. Our friend makes a shifting impression, looking at times like a romantic poet, at other times like a veteran riverboat gambler, at other times like a priest unfrocked for social indiscretions.

There is still something of the little rascal about the way he moves. He's mischievous, never pompous. He seems to be living in response to a scherzo only he hears.

He doesn't pretend indifference to money. But on the other hand, he doesn't talk like a stockbroker as some of his fellows do.

He is not impressed with kudos. When I decided in a deluded moment to take on the co-direction of the Lincoln Center Repertory Theatre he was the only friend who considered it not an honour but a personal mistake. "It's not you," he said. How right he was!

He loves all kinds of company, slips in and out of some rooms like he was breaking a rule his mother had laid down, bursting into other company with his laugh, that cackle of defiant energy.

And while now he jets instead of riding a bicycle, he is always on the move, still searching. For what? Nothing tangible. What's that line from *Camino Real*? "Make journeys. Attempt them. That's all there is!"

He lives what he speaks. His natural habitat seems to be a hotel room.

Is he reminding himself that life is temporary? He carries his own world with him.

Is he romantic? Of course. Who attached an opprobrious meaning to that word? If he deceives anyone, it is only himself.

He does not escort glamorous women of sudden wealth, he wearing dark glasses and a panama hat and giving out with profundities as he is being photographed at their side for the social page of Saturday afternoon's *New York Post*.

He has no plans to run for political office. He is not in the business of being right. When I read his work, I don't feel his elbow in my short ribs urging me to think as he does. He doesn't devote his time to straightening people out.

Mildred Dunnock in *Baby Doll* (1956).

He still lives the unscheduled life of the young man. He is openly and naturally envious of the Sweet Bird of Youth. Every chance he gets he rides on its back, wherever it may lead.

And despite his constant complaints about palpitations of the heart, he will bury us all, enduring not because he is physically better endowed than the rest of us – his exercise regime is as much from vanity as anything else – but because he is adventurous. He is brave. That brings long life. He has, in fact, lived his own life and it wasn't easy. It looks easy now, but it wasn't.

He has, an inspiration to us all, made a source of strength out of every weakness, artistic muscle out of his disabilities.

In an age when it is required of everyone to be friendly, it seems to me some special premium should be placed on friendship, the real article. I think he and I have a strong friendship though we rarely see each other.

I don't know what I've meant to him. I am trying to tell you what he has meant to me. What little I know about writing I learned more from him than from anyone. He taught me what an author is, not the writer, the artist. The spirit of the man, not his craft.

I have often wondered where this man found the nerve to stand naked before the world.

The writer when he is also an artist is someone who admits what others don't dare reveal.

In that way he becomes the spokesman for the race, for that great majority of men and women who remain silent.

What greater service is there?

I don't know.

189

Eli Wallach and Carroll Baker in *Baby Doll* (1956)

LETTERS TO TENNESSEE WILLIAMS
(About 1954–5)

Tenn, I hope this letter doesn't sound presumptuous or preachy or superior or moral – but here goes anyway. Maybe I've got no call to write anybody, because I'm kind of fucked up too in my own way. But here it is, for what it's worth. It seems to me that the very things that make it uncomfortable for you here in the States are the things that make you write. I've seen it with a lot of writers (Cliff Odets for instance) that once they had dough and the power to live in a comfortable environment (as who doesn't want to) the *necessary* quality in their writing disappeared. It seems to me that the things that make a man want to write in the first place are those elements in his environment, personal or social, that outrage him, hurt him, make him bleed. Any artist is a misfit. Why the hell would he go to all the trouble if he could make the "adjustment" in a "normal" way? In Rome, I'd say, you felt a kind of suspension of discomfort. Things are distant but, in so far as they impinge at all, not unpleasant. You start a play[1] about an American Dictator here in the States – I suppose in answer to things in our state of affairs that make it impossible for you to continue to be silent. You get to Rome or whatever and you can perfectly well remain silent. I don't think you'll ever turn out plays like Sidney Kingsley or Gar Kanin (to mention the best) purely out of ambition . . . or even in order to continue being T. Williams. You are not really Tennessee Williams in Rome. That fellow is a misfit, who was a rebel and a not-at-home in our Essentially Businessman's Society. Blanche[2] was a fragile white moth beating against the unbreakable sides of a 1000 watt bulb. But in Rome the 1000 watt bulb doesn't exist. The moth is more or less at home – especially with the checks and the Buick and all around what appears to be a gentle, softly decaying civilization. In Rome, in North Africa, in Mexico etc. your essential identity is lost. That's why I've always thought that, whether you like it or not, and in a way, especially since you do not, you should stay here in the States. I think you'd soon have some new plays writing that NO ONE could turn you off.

Love

GADGE

[1] *Sweet Bird of Youth.*

[2] Character in *A Streetcar Named Desire.*

190

A play is a dramatist catching an experience that is so intense that it changes all the characters by the time it's through. If the experience isn't that intense, the playwright has chosen the wrong incident.

What must it mean to be the son of Big Daddy?

You have to answer that, not me. You know more about it. You know a lot about it. I don't. But I do know that it means something and what it means is part of what the play is about and a part that is presently left out.

I want to see the play right first.

And I don't care who likes it. I like and respect Frank[1] and I like Chris[2] and respect his judgment. But I think what I think, baby, and I have a terrible conviction about what I think here.

And I really think there is some piece of brutal painful self-examination you haven't made yet. For instance, "What caused me to be what I am?"

Carroll Baker and Karl Malden in *Baby Doll* (1956).

[1]Tennessee Williams's friend, Frank Merlo.
[2]Christopher Isherwood.

191

THE ACTORS' STUDIO: AS I SEE US

Text of programme for an Actors' Studio benefit evening.

It has been said of us – the members of the Actors' Studio – that we are arrogant. I believe the contrary: we don't sufficiently honor ourselves. It is absolutely fitting that, at well-spaced intervals, we pause and do what we are doing tonight, acknowledge each other with pride.

Coming back from the Philippines in 1945, the world of the theatre seemed particularly bleak. There was a void where the Group Theatre had been five years before. The two great voices of the Group were silent. Harold Clurman, who'd taught us that the theatre must be a force for good in our society, was in Hollywood, a refugee. Lee Strasberg, who'd brought a new craft and a sense of dignity to all actors, was teaching quietly and modestly, as yet unrecognized for what he was.

These two men with the support and help of Cheryl Crawford had changed the lives of everyone in the theatre, but at that moment after the Second World War, few people knew it. Today many of us believe that the Group was the most seminal event in the history of the American theatre, perhaps more because of its influence than its accomplishments.

When Robert Lewis and I got together in 1946 our hope was to continue the work of the Group, to spread its influence and to keep its spirit alive. That was the first purpose of the Actors' Studio.

I ask you now to look back with me for a few moments and pay a few people the respect of remembering them.

The first reach Bobby and I made was to Cheryl Crawford. She served more than twenty years, keeping us solvent and functioning.

We opened our active life in the attic of a church devoted to actors on Forty-Seventh Street, a shelter provided us without cost. Immediately we laid down our first principle: there would be no charge for instruction. The only requirements for admission to the Studio were to be talent and desire. Actors were invited to be members by the directors because of their capabilities and their promise. That principle has been maintained for over thirty years; it still holds, it will never be otherwise. In a society where so much instruction in the arts is a racket, the Actors' Studio remains a clean place.

It was this spirit which attracted so many artists to come to us over the years and give what they had. Bobby Lewis conducted the first class of young professionals, working devotedly for two years, asking nothing except the privilege of giving of himself to a cause in which he believed. In his first class were Marlon Brando, Monty Clift, Sidney Lumet, David Wayne, Jerome Robbins, Kevin McCarthy, Eli Wallach, John Forsythe, Mildred Dunnock, Herbert Berghof, Karl Malden, E.G. Marshall, Maureen Stapleton, Beatrice Straight.

Anna Sokolow, the dancer and choreographer, a fierce and uncompromising artist, gave classes. Edith Stebbins and Alice Hermes taught speech and voice season after season. Molly Thatcher organized and operated the first playwrights' group. It continues still. Artists including Harold Clurman, Bill Inge, Edward Albee all contributed their talent and experience.

I must mention Dorothy Willard, whom I am certain few of you remember. She moved us out of our church attic and into roomier quarters. A romantic who looked like a social worker, she maintained us

The beginnings of the
Actors' Studio: the actors
of the Group Theatre
reading the cast paper.

Marlon Brando and Eva Marie Saint in *On the Waterfront* (1954).

through our early years. Eddie Kook, a good heart, provided lighting equipment. Many a movie producer helped provide us with what we required for rent, phones and secretarial services. Now we are fortunate in a new benefactor, Carl Schaeffer, a person of unique devotion and generosity.

The most important event in the development of the Studio took place when Cheryl Crawford and I, after some years of effort, succeeded in gaining the full-time participation of Lee Strasberg. Since that time, for more than two decades, he has been the embodiment of our purpose. His contribution has been above all a spiritual one: by affirming the dignity of us all as artists, he changed the life of every actor in this country whether they knew of him or not. He is our beloved artistic director.

Lee Strasberg has made the Actors' Studio a worldwide force in the performing arts.

Theatre historians are fond of saying after ten years, the Group Theatre failed – that's their word – and died. Nonsense! The Group had ten years of achievement, each year proving its point in a different way. All organisms die. What continues is the living monuments they leave behind. What the Group accomplished passed into the culture of the nation.

We who follow on are pleased to have had this influence. At the same time we are aware that there is a danger when you become the establishment. Someone has said that success in the arts is more difficult to deal with than failure. There is truth in this quip. Consider the careers of some of our playwrights, directors and actors and their over-hyped careers. What a burden the necessity of success is.

As for the schools, institutes and academies we seemed to have spawned, when money is taken for instruction in the arts, there is the inevitable danger that pupils will be accepted because they have the money to pay tuition fees and for that reason in particular. Need I say more?

What is ahead of us, the Actors' Studio? Are we at our maturity? Are we past it? Are we at the beginning of a second phase? To answer this question truthfully we must proceed to another choppy question: where have we not succeeded? What have we not done?

Are we, for instance, only a naturalistic theatre tradition? What of the plays of rhetoric and poetry? What of the classics of extra-human imagery, those works which make even our best realistic authors seem small?

Every human effort in the arts, as it succeeds in one arena, must neglect another. Every human success is simultaneously a disappointment, every triumph leaves a doubt. Could I have done it better? Should I have done it otherwise? Can I also do the other? The more we know, the less we yield to self-esteem.

Speaking for myself, I know there is so much more I could have done and should have done and what I did do I might have done better.

In the light of this self-confrontation, we realize that there is a time to move on. It is not right for an artist to work at sixty as he worked at thirty. The same goes for institutions. Other energies, other perceptions arise. Other problems must be met, other goals reached for. We survive by altering ourselves.

Artistic institutions particularly tend to become sterile as they become successful. Beware when you arrive at a point when you are not questioned. Worry when you don't ask tougher questions of yourself than others ask of you. When an actor tells me he knows just how to do a scene, I have cause for concern.

One thing about the Studio that has bothered me is how often people of talent have left before they reach the end of what is no more than the first stage of their capability. Often this departure takes place following a first great public acceptance.

People are too often satisfied when their gifts receive acknowledgment in the market place, when other people are pleased with them.

Yes, we are famous, yes, respected, envied, acclaimed. Now let's ask ourselves – since we know the reaches of our craft better than anyone else – have we fulfilled the capabilities of our talent, have we fully used our opportunity, the one we have given ourselves?

The answer to that question is always no.

That respected master whose respect we seek is lodged in ourselves.

And as we old-timers work less and in a narrower concern, as we begin the task of putting down what we have to say in books that will pass on whatever we know of worth to others, there appear new opportunities for new people. Carl Sandberg said, "There is always the young stranger."

The time for ours is coming. It may, in fact, be here. And even before these young strangers walk on our stage and go to work, I say to them, "Welcome! You have our blessing!"

THE TICK-TOCK OF TIME

Actors' Studio prize-giving dinner, November 5th, 1980.

You people must think we're nuts. There are Oscars and there are Tonys, AFI Life Achievement Awards and Kennedy Center once-in-a-lifetime awards, there are glistening Golden Globes and Silver Phalluses in carry-home sizes, Obies and an explosion of awards for every variety of country music, yes, a veritable gusher of honors, an overflow! Still here we are, apparently so avid for recognition that we call you together at a hundred and a half a plate, to watch us give still another set of prizes – to ourselves!

I'm going to try and get away with a suggestion that we are only responding to the condition of the actor in our theatre. Is that a bit heavy for you? Then try this on: being performing artists, perhaps we are extra aware of how little time we have to release our cries of pain and of rage, our murmurs of pleasure and our shouts of joy. We recognize how quickly we're gone and forgotten. We live in a dreadful apprehension that things may not get better, that no play which desperately needs us will come along, just as, in the case of a writer, the paper may remain blank; in short that our desperate push for achievement will be concluded in another blink of the cosmic eye, come up empty, out and over, *finis* to our story, the end!

So despite the fact that privately we scorn awards and sometimes publicly refuse them, they nevertheless have a secret meaning for us, one so central that we create an occasion like this one and run the risk you may think us fools.

Have you ever reflected on the life of the actor? The bottom line is that he or she has to win the favor of absolutely everyone in the wolf's circle of our theatre. Start with the director who has to be so passionately enthusiastic about her (I won't keep repeating "him or her", I'll stick to the feminine). I was saying: the director has to

like the actress candidate so dearly that he can urge her on his playwright with complete conviction.

Next, the playwright. He saw the part differently of course – they always do – so he looks the actress over very carefully, is cautious not to express any final opinion until his agent – and his wife – have had their say.

Then the producer. He has to approve, of course, approve the salary of the actress as well. If there is a star, that media-inflated balloon has to affirm, "Yes, I'll play with that actress," which is not easy for a star to say; since in time he may be held to it despite a change in his disposition.

Now the audience. They have to be viscerally interested in our actress the instant she breaks out on stage. If they are not, the author's agent, who has suddenly put in an appearance, will blame whatever is not happening with his client's play on our actress. Whispered conferences will take place in the back of the theatre and the author, who at this point, preview or try-out, is deep in doubt, will be all too ready to blame everything on everyone except himself. The easiest thing to do is change a performer, our actress for instance, just as in baseball, after an under five hundred season, the manager is sure to fall – who else?

Finally there are the critics, who know nothing about the art of acting – you may consider that an exaggeration – and have their editors to deal with, those editors who have repeatedly reminded them that they are entertainers after all and that there are only two ways to be entertaining in print, to slaughter or to worship. Anything in between is a bore.

That's a tough defensive line to break through. Our poor actress! Still she will survive somehow. We all survive. Some-

The beginnings of the Actors' Studio. Lee Strasberg, director, Elia Kazan, Tony Kraber and Michael Gordon, actors from the Group Theatre, at a summer camp in the mid 1930s.

how. But occasionally she may need a kind word and, perhaps, that momentary reassurance which comes from the ripping open of an envelope and the public reading of her name.

The central fact of the actress's life is waste, the waste of her days and her talent. By time, by inactivity, by sterile tasks, by being driven to deal with dramatic clichés only. I've watched friends persist year after year, shoulder against that great stone the poets describe, the one they dream they're pushing up a steep hill and which always rolls back to the same place. Who is more gallant, I ask you, than our actress, devoting herself season after season to her craft: speech classes, voice classes, dancing classes, scene-analysis classes, not to mention the inevitable therapist, a psychoanalyst for sure – where does she get the money?

Time doesn't stop ticking. We know it's possible nothing will get better, and oh the potential unrealized! Our young woman, struggling against the odds, will remember the day her father told her not to go for it. She will feel life slipping past her and away, like the wake of an ocean liner. And her looks! How long does the bloom bloom?

As for success, when and if it happens, it's temporary. In our theatre it is not a solution. A Broadway hit is cause for celebration until one has played it three or four months. Then there comes a kind of daze, a dum, dum, dum of meaningless repetition. Some nights our actress will manage to find her first life again. Other nights, she may wonder, as the old joke goes, "Who do I have to fuck to get out of this play?"

Meantime pride is being attacked. A danger: she may be humbled and let me tell you, our artist can't afford to be humble. Arrogance is better. She must believe she has something unique and extraordinary to give, that what she has is, in fact, irreplaceable.

Which brings me to the Actors' Studio. It was founded thirty-four years ago and is, as our world-famous artistic director Lee Strasberg likes to point out, the oldest continuing theatrical institution in this country. It was founded as a place for actors to develop their craft, but it has another purpose perhaps more basic and more profound. It is a buffer protecting the actor from the attacks on her self-esteem. The Actors' Studio by its continuance and by the words and spirit of its leader has given our actress the thing she needs most, backbone!

I've just come back from Greece, where I saw a performance of a collective of actors from Georgia, not the home of our lame duck President but a country in the federation of peoples which is Russia. The Roustabelli Troupe played Brecht in their own style, one closer than any I've ever seen to the spirit of the man I knew years ago in southern California – I can remember his mocking face stuffed with the butt of a cigar and his bright doubting eyes. The décor of this production seemed to be made up of bits of discarded scenery from other shows – or was it old farmyard fencing? The props were clumsily thrown together. The costumes gave the impression that the performers had stitched up their improvisations – not a bad idea, by the way.

But the spirit of that company overcame every seeming inadequacy. I marvelled at this integrated and totally confident group, playing Brecht like a zany operetta. I came back the next afternoon to watch the rehearsal of the change in program, *Richard III*. The work on stage, mostly marking places, moves and points, had a harmonious buzz. I talked to the director. He was proud that his government had demonstrated its esteem by sending the company to Greece. Italy was next, then Mexico and, hopefully, here. New York is still the big prize.

Those actors do not need to give themselves awards.

Meantime here in this uniquely wealthy country which is constantly squandering one of its principal resources, the talents of its artists, we languish. Even in our most modest operation on Forty-Fourth Street,

Clifford Odets, the Group Theatre's favorite playwright.

ist in America spends his youth collecting materials to build a bridge to the moon and ends by building a shack. You've all seen Orson Welles, I'm sure, assuring us with all the conviction he can muster, that a certain large corporation of wine merchants will not sell a bottle of its product before its time. Meantime, Welles himself has at least two films unfinished. Does he believe what he says about that wine? Does it matter?

Actually we don't ask for a minute of your pity. Only for some help. You know it's not easy to ask for help. I've never been able to do it. Thanks to Carl Schaeffer, who is.

But, you should also know that even without funds we would survive. One quality an artist has, because he must, is tenacity. Call it resilience.

I'll tell you a story about resilience then get off. Recently a friend, Harold Clurman, died. I went to see him in the hospital on several occasions, the last but a couple of days before his death. Harold was a man who enjoyed life. Like the rest of us, he had successes and he had failures. I don't remember seeing him humbled. He particularly loved the company of show people. The Group Theatre which he founded with Lee and Cheryl Crawford incarnated his spirit. There, in his small room at Mount Sinai hospital, a few weeks ago, people who'd heard the news came visiting in a constant flow. They didn't find a man mired in self-pity. Although pneumonia had set in and he had to lie for twenty minutes on one side then be turned over to the other, he lay on his pillow, a gentle smile on his soft fleshy features, looking at his visitors with a welcoming affection.

The day I came for the last time there was a discussion going on between Harold and his second wife. The subject? The relation of justice to compassion. Justice had to be unassailable, of course, but compassion has to be ready at hand, always. It was the kind of abstract weighing of values French intellectuals enjoy: as a young man Harold studied at the Sorbonne.

Occasionally his mind seemed to drift off.

expenses are not met unless, each year, we dream up a stunt like this one to pay for light, heat, a telephone and a secretary. One hundred and fifty dollars? We could use more. We try to gauge your limits. We've probably hit it right; the joint is full tonight.

So, instead of having the strength which comes from the support of our society as a whole, we scrounge from you, our friends, and hope for the best.

Clifford Odets, a man given to romantic images which may sound a bit puffy in these drabber days, once said that the art-

Left: Elia Kazan with Katharine Hepburn, during the shooting of *The Sea of Grass* (1946).
Right: Elia Kazan with Jeanne Crain, during the shooting of *Pinky* (1949).

Overleaf: Elia Kazan with Marlon Brando.
Top: shooting *A Streetcar Named Desire* (1950).
Bottom: shooting *On the Waterfront* (1954).
Right: shooting *Viva Zapata!* (1951).

Opposite: Elia Kazan with Andy Griffith and Lee Remick during the shooting of *A Face in the Crowd* (1956).
Elia Kazan with Julie Harris, during the shooting of *East of Eden* (1954).
Elia Kazan with James Dean, during the shooting of *East of Eden* (1954).
Elia Kazan with Karl Malden and Carroll Baker, during the shooting of *Baby Doll* (1956).

207

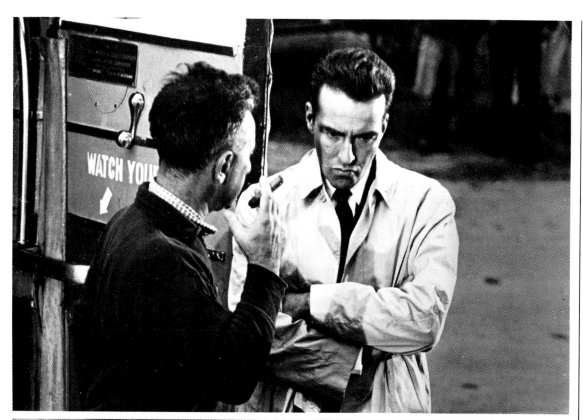

Elia Kazan and
Montgomery Clift during
the shooting of *Wild River*
(1960).

Overleaf: Elia Kazan with
Patricia Neal and Andy
Griffith, during the
shooting of *A Face in the
Crowd* (1956).

Elia Kazan with Jo Van
Fleet, during the shooting
of *Wild River* (1960).

Elia Kazan and Natalie
Wood, during the shooting
of *Splendor in the Grass*
(1960).

Elia Kazan and Stathis
Giallelis, during the
shooting of *America
America* (1964).
Elia Kazan and Richard
Boone, during the
shooting of *The
Arrangement* (1969).

Overleaf: (left) Elia Kazan
with Faye Dunaway and
Kirk Douglas, during the
shooting of *The
Arrangement* (1969).
(*Right, top to bottom*) Elia
Kazan with James Woods
and Chico Martinez,
during the shooting of *The
Visitors* (1971); with Jack
Nicholson during the
shooting of *The Last
Tycoon* (1976); and with
Jeanne Moreau and Robert
De Niro (*The Last Tycoon*)
(1976).

211

He must have been wondering about the final gravity of his illness because he twice asked me if I ever got sick. I assured him I was mortal and had known bad days. Later I watched the daughter of his first wife tenderly stroking his head, a baby to her hand, and noted how he looked at her, such joy at her caress.

It was then the thought occurred to me that Harold Clurman, who'd hugely enjoyed everything in his life from a lobster dinner to the rehearsals of a play he knew had no chance for commercial success, was now enjoying the occasion of his death. His death, it seemed, was a binding of his friends. He died in a harmony with the people he loved.

Had he achieved all he might have? Have any of us? Perhaps he did not. Writing criticism and teaching acting was not, in the end, what he most wanted to do. He wanted to be part of what seems to be impossible here, part of a *continuing* group, a Group Theatre. That did not happen for him. Still he left his mark on all of us, even those too young to remember him in his prime.

We all know that terrible sentence, I might have done more! We've experienced it. We are apprehensive about it. Giving prizes is silly, sure, and giving them to ourselves – well! But when that ritual begins, my friends, perhaps you will have some idea now of why we take part in it.

The question I am asked most often by interviewers is, "Who was the best actor with whom you worked?" which is certainly a stupid question. We rate prize fighters, one, two, three and tennis players, but artists cannot be scaled, best, second best and so on. They can only hope to be themselves. An actor can be good in one role and very poor in the next. It is quite impossible for him or her to excel unless the part is well conceived, well written and ably supported. And the director does not commit excesses and narcissistic foolishness. So let's not talk about the "best".

Nevertheless the best actor I've worked with was Marlon Brando and I feel certain that this judgment in this case would be

supported by all the competition. It is the only case of an artist in my time whose selection for the top of the heap would receive the concurrence of all the others in his field. Marlon had everything. Not only was he, at one time, the most beautiful man in films, both in face and body, but he had all the essential talents. He had emotion of a terrifying and awesome intensity. He had great imagination but never eccentric, that is to say always within the bounds of reality. He had an astonishing ability to characterize a role – compare his brilliant performance in *Godfather One* and the one he gave in *Zapata*. He was a great mimic, could astonish with his voice as well as with his postures. He had an abundant and always ready humor. And he was capable of surprise – the dearest quality an actor can have for his director: he was able to carry out an instruction so that it was better than what the director was hoping for. With Brando the director was always hoping for a miracle and he often got it. Finally he had

Pat Hinge and Warren Beatty in *Splendor in the Grass* (1960).

Marlon Brando in *A Streetcar Named Desire* (1950).

213

Elia Kazan, Marlon Brando (visiting), Julie Harris and James Dean, during the shooting of *East of Eden* (1954).

what few actors have, a surprising intelligence. He would understand a role, yes, but also the theme and direction of an entire production. He was a true collaborator too. I have many feelings as I remember him, but perhaps the chief one is gratitude for what he contributed to my films.

The most intelligent actor I've worked with after Marlon is – and this may surprise you – Warren Beatty. Less an actor than a personality, he does not have the surprising gift that Marlon has of transforming himself. He is actually of an older and more old-fashioned tradition: he "comes on" as himself. He is always "straight" and he never surprises. But he has exceptional courage as a man, or you might say fear-

lessness. I admire him very much for making *Reds*. I don't know anyone else who would have done it. And there are elements in all his films that shock and surprise. But whereas Brando has great actor's technique, Warren does not. What he does have is sex appeal – not a quality to be scorned in a performer. He is abundantly masculine where Marlon is fully sexed but uni-sexed. Warren appeals to women. I believe that in time he will become a hyphenate, a producer-director. And do very well, for he is loaded with enterprise and daring. These are rare qualities in our cinema and I esteem him for them.

James Dean in *East of Eden* (1954).

216

Montgomery Clift in *Wild River* (1960).

James Dean and Julie Harris in *East of Eden* (1954).

The actor I've worked with who had the most natural talent after Marlon was Jimmy Dean. But he lacked technique; he had no proper training. He could not play a part outside of his age range. He often hit a scene immediately and instinctively right. Sometimes he did not and then there would be problems. Nor was his intelligence of a high order. Directing him was gratifying because he always caught something of the spirit of the youth which considered itself disenfranchised by the preceding generation, their parents. But there was an element of self-pity here and I found this irksome. He had considerable violence but not as an adjunct of strength or courage, but of hatred and a kind of despair. His imagination was limited; it was like a child's. To direct him was somewhat like directing Lassie the dog; the director dealt in a series of rewards and threats and played a psychological game with him. He had to be coddled and hugged or threatened with abandonment. His own favorite actor was Brando and the only word possible here is hero-worship. When Brando came to visit my set of *East of Eden*, Jimmy was awestruck and nearly shrivelled with respect. But I cannot concur in an impression that has some currency, that he fell into Marlon's mannerisms; he had his own and they were ample.

He was fortunate in *East of Eden* that he had with him one of the young saints of the American theatre, Julie Harris, an actress who had all of Marlon's gifts but on a miniature scale. She also had emotional force wedded, as Marlon's was, to gentleness. Two of the most gentle scenes in my films are the scenes Marlon played with Eva Marie Saint (another angel) in *On the Waterfront* and the one Julie played at the end of *East of Eden* which is – I speak of her performance – of surprising beauty. She also brought to that production the quality I needed most to help with Jimmy Dean, kindly patience. I believe that most any

Lee Remick in *Wild River* (1960).

Frank Overton and Montgomery Clift in *Wild River* (1960).

218

Kirk Douglas and Richard
Boone in *The Arrangement*
(1969).

other actress would have time and again become restless and even resentful of the psychological games Dean played. But not Julie. She made Jimmy feel that he was a first-class artist and he flowered under her encouragement.

Montgomery Clift I knew in the prime of his youth in my stage play, *Skin of Our Teeth* and after his accident in *Wild River*. One quality survived the terrible accident on the hill down from Elizabeth Taylor's house: a sensitivity so complete that it rather unmanned him. He quivered with emotion and this was not generally useful. Opposite him in *Wild River* was a marvellous woman (I've been, generally speaking, more fortunate in my actresses than in my actors), a beauty who combined that with strength, Lee Remick. While Clift was trembling with uncertainty, she was a stalwart. The result was a shift of the roles – correct for the story of *Wild River*. The

woman became the strong one, the man the uncertain one. I don't know what Clift's appeal was – he certainly had a good deal – but it was not sexual. I believe it was that which an orphan has; he called for help. Lee gave it to him. She ably represented everything that we regard as worthy and honorable in the tradition of our country. She was also a great beauty, in fact, for a time, a perfect beauty, one without a flaw. She was not outstandingly talented but she had a sweet and estimable quality. A man is lucky when he finds a woman as good and so decent. A woman who finds herself with Clift may or may not consider herself fortunate; she will certainly find herself overwhelmed with the problems of a wounded psyche. Clift was sexually ambivalent. At the same time he was a young man with honor and uprightness. When he was in his late teens he found the sympathy he wanted in my wife, Molly. He used to come to my house and sit at her feet and seek a replacement for – I had to suppose – his mother. When he came to work on *Wild River* he brought a dramatic coach on the set and she stood at the back and then later, in their apartment, would advise him, in fact rehearse him, in his next day's work. I was able to insist that the lady, Mira Roskoya, not come on the set but I didn't try to prevent the consultations they had at night. He was a wounded man then and I must say my impression was that Mira preyed on his hurts; they provided her with an opportunity to shine. In the production Lee did the best she could with the scenes of physical love, but they were never what I hoped for. One critical scene I rehearsed then decided to never bring the camera close; I left it in long shot.

The most colorful and unswerving personality I ever worked with was Andy Griffith. He was "strictly country" in every way and in most of *A Face in the Crowd* this served delightfully. There were a few scenes of more dramatic intent where I relied on the help of strong drink; we called it the JACK DANIELS SCHOOL OF ACTING to distinguish it from the Stanislavsky Method School. It is the one occasion, I believe, where I cast for the "real thing", a personality, not an actor. He rewarded Budd Schulberg and me with the performance we needed.

The other actor I've worked with who had great intelligence and a kind of permanent bravado was Kirk Douglas. My God, he was intelligent! But he lacked an essential for the kind of films I was making: vulnerability. It was impossible to believe that he would ever lose anything, a war or a love contest, anything! This rather deflates the essential conflict of the film I made with him. It had nothing to do with Kirk's intelligence. He understood what I wanted. But his genes didn't permit him to experience – or demonstrate – before the camera the emotional effect I needed.

The actress I most admired, along with Julie Harris, was Geraldine Page. She could do anything – once she knew what it was you wanted and once you gave her the courage which comes from the director's absolute certainty that she could do what he was calling for. I would say that she had many of the qualities one hopes for in a theatre artist to a degree that was surprising and she did two plays of Tennessee Williams better than anyone else could have.

An interesting contrast is the one between the two women who played Blanche DuBois in *A Streetcar Named Desire*. Jessica Tandy, who played the role on stage, was the completely trained actress in the tradition of the English dramatic academies. She knew her business, how to work, how to produce the results. She was – and is – a fine woman and this always shows. She appreciated the humanity of her role and conducted herself on stage perfectly to project this. Vivien Leigh was a complex woman and a fascinating one. She could be compared only to a cat; she had a small talent but a considerable intelligence, and the greatest determination I've ever seen in an actress. She would do anything – crawl through broken glass, I used to say – if it was good for the role. She resisted me a great deal at first since she'd already played the role on the British stage under the direction of her husband, Larry Olivier. But I had another taste and a different disposition; I made other demands for other spiritual effects. She soon accepted my challenges and rose to meet them. I think she is rather artificial in the first two reels and I was disappointed. But in what followed, I admired what she did.

There is no such thing as a definite performance of a masterpiece. There is no definitive performance of the role of Blanche DuBois. The role was played by two fine actresses but could have been played equally well by Geraldine Page and Julie Harris and Kim Stanley. *Chacun à son goût.* I might have liked them all – those others – but I don't wish I had seen them. My memory of the two performances I had a part in producing is ample for me; I don't want it disturbed which is why I do not see any other performances of this play or of any other play I've done.

It is one of the curses of our theatre, I suppose, that with some sort of perverted respect for the star system, we only talk about "Leading men" and "Leading ladies", that is "stars". But I have never been more grateful to any actor than to Lee Cobb, who played the first *Death of a Salesman*. He

Marlon Brandon et Vivien
Leigh dans *Un tramway
nommé Désir* (1950).

Barbara Loden in *Splendor in the Grass* (1960).

was historic! Or to Karl Malden, who played so many roles for me so well. Or to Eli Wallach, Paul Newman, Chris Plummer, Milly Dunnock, Carroll Baker, Arthur Kennedy, Pat Hingle, Dick Widmark and, perhaps above all, Peggy Ann Garner.

And the actress who had a talent equal to all the others (with the same single exception, Marlon) was Barbara Loden. But she was delinquent in other respects, which was most unfortunate. She had very little range and a poor voice and this cost her. But when she was within her limits, as in Miller's play, *After the Fall*, she brought an awesome emotional power as well as an abundant humor to the role. I can't imagine anyone doing it as well. But outside her range – that of a young woman who never really matured – she would not succeed. She was a kind of genius within very narrow bounds.

I apologize to those I don't mention. I only consider the ones who came to my mind today. But there were others I esteemed; I loved them all (except Tallulah Bankhead) and I hope they will accept my apology with my ardent salute. Especially those of outstanding talent whom life and the exigencies of our theatre and film never provided the opportunities they deserved. I particularly recall Paul Mann, who was so superb in *America America*. He deserved better opportunities than those he received. There are others whom life and career have treated shamefully and I can only wish that they had been more fortunate. I cannot imagine any career that is more rewarding in its peaks and less rewarding, particularly in our country, when those peaks are not reached.

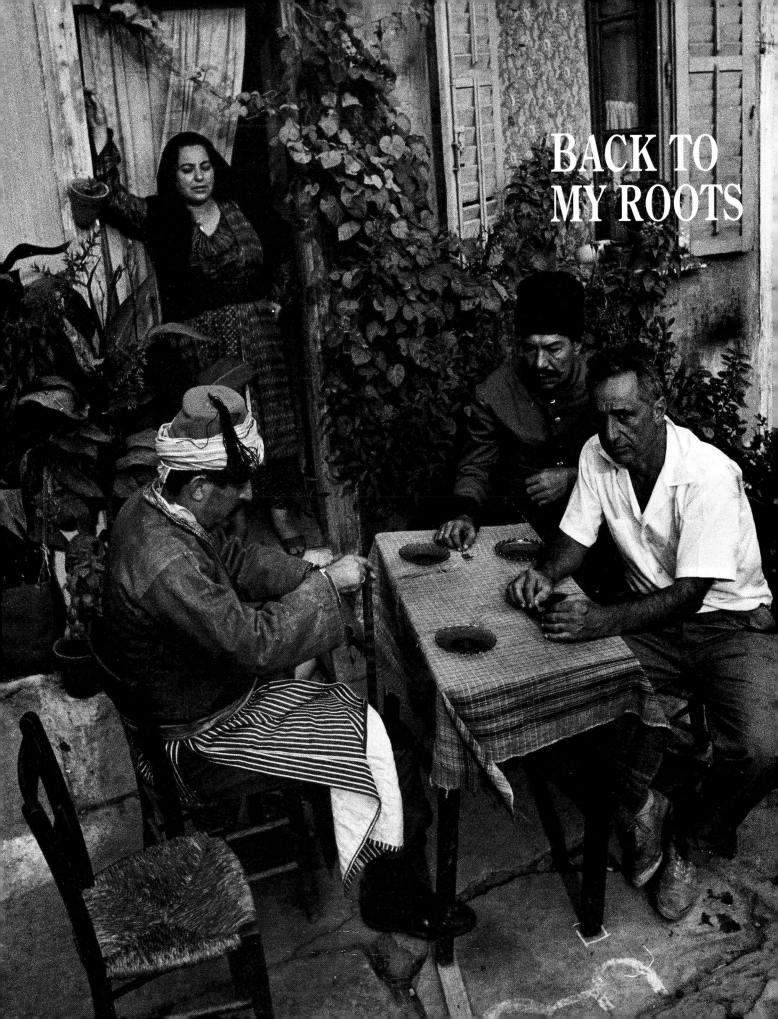

BACK TO
MY ROOTS

FAMILY PORTRAITS

The Kanzanjoglou family in Istanbul at the beginning of the century.

The Topouzoglou family in *America America* (1964).

Overleaf: shooting *America America* (1964).
Opposite: Athena and George Kanzanjoglou, Elia Kazan's parents.
Elia Kazan as a child.
Elia Kazan with his uncle Seraphin.
Elia Kazan with his younger brother Avraam.

226

MY RELATIONSHIP WITH THE USA

Speech given in Athens in April 1978.

I have been wondering why I am here, why I accepted an invitation from the USIA to come and stand up for nine of my films. I never see my old films. There are movies of mine about to be unreeled here that I have not seen since I finished them many years ago. I will not see them while I am here; I prefer not to look back.

So why? One reason, of course, is that it's a free trip to a country I love – *Hellada*! – and a chance to see relatives and friends whom I miss seeing more often. It is also a chance to give my son and my grandson, who are here with me, a glimpse of Greece and perhaps make them more aware that they are, in a vital part – their spirits – part Greek. My grandson is eleven and I know he will never forget this trip with his grandfather.

I wish I could come here more often. I have dreamed of living here part of each year. Once I almost bought a small home on the road to Navpleon, one of the most beautiful cities I know. But I keep being busier in America than I mean to be and have to squeeze in visits when and how I can. I don't want to lose my connection with you. I fear that if I don't strengthen our ties at regular intervals, they will unravel and weaken. I am determined to remain what I am. Born Greek.

So for me this visit hasn't much to do with showing off my films. I am proud of them, but they are part of my past. I hope you will enjoy them, but they no longer hold a place in my own feelings. They were made in another time by another man.

I have also wondered why the United States government chose to go to the expense of bringing us here – three generations of Kazanjioglous. Perhaps they want to demonstrate that a Greek can thrive in the United States. But that's well known, isn't it?

A Greek can get along anywhere, he always has. We have never been afraid of the sea or of strangers. Wherever we've gone we've brought a piece of our culture, set it to growing like a plant. We never surrender our identity.

My grandmother, so she told me, when she first came to New York City in 1915 brought her own yogurt culture. The first thing she did, after she walked into the apartment my father had found for her, was to make her own yogurt. Do you believe that story? My grandmother was an Anatolian, therefore a mythmaker, but perhaps it's true. Certainly there never was a day in her house or in my mother's when there weren't half a dozen tumblers of yogurt cooling in the refrigerator. I was brought up tasting this bond with the old country; we had yogurt with every meal. We used English in the streets and at school, we spoke Greek at home. We were never allowed to forget that we came from another civilization, our true mother.

European critics have noticed a certain ambivalence in my work. Am I really an American, they have asked, or am I a European, a Greek? Which?

There is an odd thing about my films, now that I look back from a perspective. They are more highly praised in Europe than they are in America. Many of them, since recognized – excuse my quoting this, I did not choose the word – as classics were disasters in the United States when they first appeared. It is these films in particular, like neglected children, of which I am most fond. You will be seeing some of them here.

For instance, *America America*, the story of how an Anatolian Greek boy managed to reach America and what he had to do to get there was a financial failure in America. *The Arrangement*, a favorite of the French, was

a complete disaster. *Viva Zapata!*, which was shown in your neighborhoods nine times one summer, lost a fortune in the States. One of my favorite films is *Wild River*, the story of how electric power, light itself, was brought to a backward area of the United States by the Federal Government program called the Tennessee Valley Authority. It is the only film that I know of about the bloodless revolution of the 1930s called the New Deal. This film was hardly shown in the United States, but it is still shown time and time again in Paris and was voted by a leading critic there one of the twenty best films of all time – an honor it doesn't deserve but I'm glad to have for it.

Why this discrepancy of tastes?

Is it because the American public, used to being entertained without being disturbed, finds something prickly in my work? I have just written a novel which will appear in our book stores in July. Before I left New York, I had a talk with my publisher, who informed me that the people who'd read the book in advance found it – the same word – too disturbing. My publisher was taking sympathetic pains to prepare me for the book's failure in the market place. I told him not to worry; I am old and have calluses on places once tender. It's always nice to be praised but I am used to being attacked, in fact I rather enjoy it. It's also nice to be proud of your failures and live in the conviction, as I have permitted myself to live, that films and books which are con-

Elia Kazan with his bodyguard Salih Tekim (*left*) visiting Yilmaz Guney in Topkapi prison (1978).

sidered failures at one time may be appreciated at another.

The fact is that from the earliest time I can remember I have had an ambivalent relationship with the United States. *Love-hate* one critic called it. I have put a harsh light on many social injustices. *A Face in the Crowd*, which you are going to see, was the first film to attack the big business of advertising. It was also a failure. It has also come back.

Now to speak personally, I have, on the one hand, been deeply grateful for the opportunities the United States has given me, and for the freedom which even in the worst of times was more generous to opposition and more open to criticism than that of any other land I know of. On the other hand, I have never been totally able to keep my mouth shut, so I speak. Not, I believe, in any ritualistic and predictable way, nor in favor of another kind of culture. But simply to say and say again that the United States is a civilization in process, that it has distance to travel and that one way it can continue to press forward is for people who are able to articulate their feelings, in one medium or another, that is to say its artists, to bear frank witness to their experience.

The problem is to expose what's bad without slighting the good, to praise the good without concealing what is bad. Ambivalence in art is hard to manage; it makes dramatic clarity difficult. It's easier to deal in black villains and innocent heroes.

In my own view, the solution is to talk about human beings and not about abstracts, to reveal the culture and the social moment as it is reflected in the behavior and the lives of individual people.

Not to be "correct". To be total.

So I do not believe in any ideology that does not permit – no encourage – the freedom of the individual.

It's inevitable that there will be bad times in the years of a democracy, there will even be moral chaos from time to time.

How can anyone feel unashamed when attack planes and shells crossing each other in opposite directions are labeled "Made in the USA"?

The United States is still a country which has not lived up to its ideals. Or to be more generous, a country which is in a process of living up to its ideals.

It is also a country trying to do the impossible.

Will it?

The answer to that question is another question.

Will we, mankind, ever, I mean the human animal, will we ever?

I think you and I, all of us, have some sort of stake in the United States. If it fails, the failure will be that of us all. Of mankind itself. It will cost us all.

Can we make a go of it as free individuals in a free society?

I don't know. I have doubted it and I have believed it.

It's an issue that will be decided – if such issues are ever decided – long after I am dead. But it is an issue of critical concern to us all.

I think of the United States as a country which is an arena and in that arena there is a drama being played out and the protagonists are not always sympathetic figures and the light where they perform their actions is murky and we often see that they are not the best of all possible acts. But even in the worst of times, I have seen that the struggle is the struggle of free men. Mistakes are made. There are tragedies. Shameful episodes. Betrayals. But the struggle continues. It seems to me that sooner or later, to some extent or another, the mistakes are corrected. We fight with each other, we embrace, we hate, we love. We have outbreaks of what amount to civil wars. The wounds heal. Through pain and conflict, there is growth. Perhaps that is the only way, through pain and through conflict. I think so.

What inhabits my films, I hope, is a reflection of this temper and of that struggle.

Opposite: Elia Kazan, during the shooting of *America America* (1964).

Overleaf: The People of the Cumberland (1937), the first film that Elia Kazan collaborated in.

231

FILMOGRAPHY

ACTOR

1934 CAFÉ UNIVERSAL
Direction: Ralph Steiner. *Short film.* Cast: Elia Kazan, Art Smith, Morris Carnovsky, Harold Clurman, Robert Lewis, Clifford Odets, Paula Strasberg.

1934 PIE IN THE SKY
Direction: Ralph Steiner. *Short film:* 10 minutes. *Cast:* Elman Koalish, Elia Kazan, Molly Day Thatcher.

1940 CITY FOR CONQUEST
Direction: Anatol Litvak. *Main character:* Googie, a gangster. *Cast:* James Cagney, Ann Sheridan, Anthony Quinn, Arthur Kennedy, Frank McHugh.

1941 BLUES IN THE NIGHT
Direction: Anatol Litvak. *Main character:* a clarinettist. *Cast:* Priscilla Lane, Richard Whorf, Betty Field.

DIRECTOR

Before Hollywood

1937 THE PEOPLE OF THE CUMBERLAND
Short film: 20 minutes. *Production:* Frontier Films. *Screenplay:* Elia Kazan. *Photography:* Ralph Steiner. *Cast:* non-professionals.

1941 IT'S UP TO YOU
Length: 2 hours. *Production:* Ministry of Agriculture. *Screenplay:* Arthur Arent. *Music:* Earl Robinson. *Cast:* Helen Tamiris.

Hollywood and after

1944 A TREE GROWS IN BROOKLYN
Screenplay: Tess Slesinger and Frank Davis, after the novel by Betty Smith. *Photography:* Leon Shamroy. *Music:* Alfred Newman. *Design:* Lyle R. Wheeler (a.d.), Thomas Little (s.d.). *Editing:* Dorothy Spencer. *Spec. Eff.* Fred Sersen. *Costumes:* Bonnie Cassin. *Production:* Louis D. Lighton, Twentieth-Century Fox. 128 mn. *Cast:* Dorothy McGuire (Kathy Nolan), Joan Blondell (Aunt Sissy), James Dunn (Johnny Nolan), Lloyd Nolan (Det. McShayne), Peggy Ann Garner (Francie Nolan), Ted Donaldson (Neely Nolan), James Gleason (McGarrity), Ruth Nelson (Miss McDonohough), John Alexander (Steve Edwards), J. Farrell McDonald (Garney), B.S. Pully (Christmas tree salesman), Charles Halton (Mr Barker), Art Smith (ice-cream man), Ferike Bozos (Grandma Rommely), Lillian Bronson (bookseller), Peter Cusanelli (barber), Adeline de Walt Reynolds (Mrs Waters), George Melford (Mr Spencer), Mae Marsh, Edna Jackson (the Timmore sisters), Vincent Graeff (Henry Gaddis), Susan Lester (Flossie Gaddis), Johnnie Barnes (Mr Grackenbox), Alec Craig (Werner), Al Bridge (Charlie), Joseph J. Greene (Hassler), Virginia Brissac (Miss Tilford), Harry Harvey Jr (Herschel), Robert Andersen (Angie), Erskine Sanford (undertaker), Martha Wentworth (the mother), Francis Pierlot (the priest).

1946 THE SEA OF GRASS
Screenplay: Marguerite Roberts and Vincent Lawrence, after the novel by Conrad Richter. *Photography:* Harry Stradling. *Music:* Herbert Stothart. *Design:* Cedric Gibbons, Paul Groesse (a.d.), Edwin B. Willis, Mildred Griffiths (s.d.). *Editing:* Robert J. Kern. *Spec. Eff.:* A. Arnold Gillespie, Warren Newcombe. *Costumes:* Walter Plunkett. *Production:* Pandro S. Berman, M.G.M. 131 mn. *Cast:* Spencer Tracy (Colonel Jim Brewton), Katharine Hepburn (Lutie Cameron), Melvyn Douglas (Brice Chamberlain), Robert Walker (Brock Brewton), Phylis Thaxter (Sarah Beth Brewton), Edgar Buchanan (Jeff), Harry Carey (Dr Reid), Ruth Nelson (Selina Hall), Robert Armstrong (Floyd McCurtin), James Bell (Sam Hall), Charles Trowbridge (George Cameron), Russell Hicks (Major Harney), Morris Ankrum (Crane), Robert Barratt (White), William Phipps (Brandy), Trevor Bardette (Andy Boggs).

1946 BOOMERANG
Screenplay: Richard Murphy, after the article "The Perfect Case" by Anthony Abbott (penname of Fulton Oursler). *Photography:* Norbert Brodine. *Music:* David Buttolph. *Design:* Richard Day, Chester Gore, Thomas Little (s.d.). *Editing:* Harmon Jones. *Spec. Eff.:* Fred Sersen. *Production:* Louis De Rochemont, Twentieth-Century Fox. 88 mn. *Cast:* Dana Andrews (Henry L. Harvey), Jane Wyatt (Mrs Harvey), Lee J. Cobb (Robinson), Sam Levene (Woods), Cara Williams (Irene Nelson), Arthur Kennedy (John Waldron), Robert Keith (McGreery), Taylor Holmes (Wade), Leona Roberts (Mrs Grossman), Philip Coolidge (Grossman), Ben Lackland (James), Ed Begley (Harris), Wyley Birch (Father Lambert), Karl Malden (Lt White), Lester Lonergan (Gary), Lewis Leverett (Whitney), Barry Kelley (Sgt Dugan), Richard Garrick (Mr Rogers), Richard Murphy, Joe Kazan (Mr Lukash), Ida McGuire (Miss Roberts), Clay Clement (Judge Tate), Helen Carew (Annie), Johnny Stearns (Rev. Gardiner), Guy Thomajan (Cartucci), Lucia Segher (Mrs Lukash), George Petrie (O'Shea), John Carmody (Callahan), E. J. Ballantine (McDonald), William Chaclee (Stone), Edgar Stehli (Colonel), Jimmy Dobson (Bill), Bernard Hoffman (Tom), Lee Roberts (criminal), Pauline Myers (girl), Jacob Sandler (barman), Herbert Rather (investigator), Fred Stewart (Graham), Lawrence Paquin (sheriff), Anna Minot (secretary), Dudley Sadler (Dr Rainsford), Walter Greaza (Mayor Swayze), Helen Hatch (Miss Manion).

1947 GENTLEMAN'S AGREEMENT
Screenplay: Moss Hart, after the novel by Laura Z. Hobson. *Photography:* Arthur Miller. *Music:* Alfred Newman. *Design:* Lyle R. Wheeler, Mark-Lee Kirk (a.d.), Thomas Little, Paul S. Fox (s.d.). *Editing:* Harmon Jones. *Spec. Eff.:* Fred Sersen. *Costumes:* Kay Nelson, Charles Le Maire. *Production:* Darryl F. Zanuck, Twentieth-Century Fox. 118 mn. Gregory Peck (Phil Green), Dorothy McGuire (Kathy Lacey), John Garfield (Dave Goldmann), Celeste Holm (Anne Dettrey), Anne Revere (Mrs Green), Dean Stockwell (Tommy Green), Albert Dekker (John Minifee), June Havoc (Elaine Wales), Jane Wyatt (Jane), Nicholas Joy (Dr William Craigie), Sam Jaffe (Father Liebermann), Harold Vermilyea (Lou Jordan), Robert Warwick (Sterling White), Victor Kilian (Olsen), Ranson S. Sherman (Bill Payson), Roy Roberts (Mr Calkins), Curt Conway (Bert McAnny), John Newland (Bill), Louise Lorimer (Miss Miller), Howard Negley (Tingler), Frank Wilcox (Harry), Wilton Graff (waiter), Morgan Farley (employee), Kathleen Lockhart (Mrs Minifee), Marilyn Monk (receptionist).

1949 PINKY
Screenplay: Philip Dunne and Dudley Nichols, after the novel *Quality* by Cid Rickets Summer. *Photography:* Joe MacDonald. *Music:* Alfred Newman. *Design:* Lyle R. Wheeler, J. Russell Spencer (a.d.), Thomas Little, Walter M. Scott (s.d.). *Editing:* Harmon Jones. *Costumes:*

Charles Le Maire. *Production:* Darryl F. Zanuck, Twentieth-Century Fox. 102 mn. John Ford had begun *Pinky,* but after a few days' shooting he backed out, for reasons that remain obscure (illness, disagreement with Zanuck), and Kazan took over the film, re-shooting all the scenes that Ford had directed. *Cast:* Jeanne Crain (Pinky Johnson), Ethel Barrymore (Miss Em), Ethel Waters (Granny Dicey Johnson), William Lundigan (Dr Thomas Adams), Basil Ruysdael (John Walters), Kenny Washington (Dr Canady), Nina Mae McKinney (Rozelia Walters), Griff Barnett (Dr Joe), Frederick O'Neal (Jake Walters), Evelyn Warden (Melba Wooley), Raymond Greenleaf (Judge Shoreham), Dan Riss (Stanley), William Hansen (Mr Goolby), Arthur Hunnicutt (police chief).

1950 PANIC IN THE STREETS

Screenplay: Richard Murphy, after Daniel Fuchs's adaptation of a theme by Edward and Edna Anhalt. *Photography:* Joe MacDonald. *Music:* Alfred Newman. *Design:* Lyle R. Wheeler, Maurice Ransford (a.d.), Thomas Little, Fred J. Rode (s.d.). *Editing:* Harmon Jones. *Spec. Eff.:* Fred Sersen. *Costumes:* Charles Le Maire. *Production:* Sol C. Siegel, Twentieth-Century Fox. 96 mn. *Cast:* Richard Widmark (Dr Clinton Reed), Paul Douglas (Captain Warren), Barbara Bel Geddes (Nancy Reed), Walter Jack Palance (Blackie), Zero Mostel (Fitch), Dan Riss (Neff), Alexis Minotis (John Mefaris), Guy Thomajan (Poldi), Tommy Cook (Vince), Edward Kennedy (Jordan), H.T. Tsiang (cook), Lewis Charles (Kochak), Ray Muller (Dubin), Tommy Rettig (Tommy), Lenka Peterson (Jeanette), Pat Walshe (Pat), Paul Hostetler (Dr Gafney), George Ehmig (Kleber), Joseph Schilleci (Lee), Waldo Pitkin (Ben), Leo Zinser (Sgt Pelps), Beverly C. Brown (Dr McKay), Emile Meyer (Beauclyde), William A. Dean, H. Waller Fowler Jr, Red Noad, Val Winter, Wilson Bourg Jr, Tiger Joe Marsh.

1950 A STREETCAR NAMED DESIRE

Screenplay: Tennessee Williams, after Oscar Saul's adaptation of his play. *Photography:* Harry Stradling. *Music:* Alex North. *Design:* Richard Day (a.d.), George James Hopkins (s.d.). *Editing:* David Weisbart. *Costumes:* Lucinda Ballard. *Production:* Charles K. Feldman, Charles K. Feldman Group Productions. Warner Bros. 122 mn. Oscars for Richard Day (art director), George James Hopkins (set designer), Vivien Leigh (best actress), Kim Hunter (best supporting actress), Karl Malden (best supporting actor). *Cast:* Vivien Leigh (Blanche DuBois), Marlon Brando (Stanley Kowalski), Kim Hunter (Stella Kowalski), Karl Malden (Harold Mitchell, Mitch), Rudy Bond

(Steve Hubbell), Nick Dennis (Pablo Gonzales), Peg Hillias (Eunice Hubbell), Wright King (young conductor), Richard Garrick (doctor), Anne Dere (nurse), Edna Thomas (Mexican woman), Mickey Kuhn (sailor).

1951 VIVA ZAPATA!

Screenplay: John Steinbeck, after the book *Zapata the Unconquerable* by Edgcumb Pichon. *Photography:* Joe MacDonald. *Music:* Alex North. *Design:* Lyle R. Wheeler, Leland Fuller (a.d.), Thomas Little, Claude Carpenter (s.d.). *Editing:* Barbara McLean. *Costumes:* Travilla, Charles Le Maire. *Production:* Darryl F. Zanuck, Twentieth-Century Fox. 113 mn. or 125 mn. Oscar for Anthony Quinn (best supporting actor). *Cast:* Marlon Brando (Emiliano Zapata), Jean Peters (Josefa Espejo), Anthony Quinn (Eufemio Zapata), Joseph Wiseman (Fernando Aguirre), Arnold Moss (Don Nacio de la Torre), Lou Gilbert (Pablo), Alan Reed (Pancho Villa), Margo (Posedera), Harold Gordon (Francisco Madero), Mildred Dunnock (Señora Espejo), Frank Silvera (General Huerta), Nina Valera (Tia Josefa), Florenz Ames (Señor Espejo), Bernie Gozier (Zapatistia), Frank De Kova (Colonel Jesús Guardajo), Fay Roope (Porfirio Diaz), Abner Biberman (captain), Harry Kingston (Don Garcia), Wil Kuluva (Lázaro), Joseph Granby (General Fuerta), Pedro Gegas (Inocente), Richard Garrick (old general), Ross Bagdasarian (officer), Leonard George (Maeido), Fernand Eliseu (Fuentes's wife), Lisa Fusaro (Garcia's wife), Brile Mitchel (Nacio's wife).

1952 MAN ON A TIGHTROPE

Screenplay: Robert Sherwood, after the short story *International Incident* by Neil Paterson. *Photography:* Georg Krause. *Music:* Franz Waxman. *Songs:* Bert Reisfeld. *Design:* Hans H. Kuhnert, Theo Zwirsky. *Editing:* Dorothy Spencer. *Production:* Gerd Oswald for Robert L. Jacks, Twentieth-Century Fox. 105 mn. Shot in Germany. *Cast:* Fredric March (Karel Cernik), Gloria Grahame (Zama Cernik), Terry Moore (Tereza Cernik), Cameron Mitchell (Joe Vosdek), Richard Boone (Krofta), Paul Hartman (Jaromir), Pat Henning (Konradin), Alexander D'Arcy (Rudolph), the dwarf Hansi (Kalka), Dorothea Wieck (the Duchess), Adolphe Menjou (police officer Fesker), Robert Beatty (Barovic), John Dehner (the chef), William Castello (the captain), Margaret Slezak (orchestra director), Edelweiss Malchin (Vina), Philip Kenelly (the sergeant), and the Brumbach Circus.

1954 ON THE WATERFRONT

Screenplay: Budd Schulberg, after a series of articles by Malcolm Johnson. *Photography:* Boris Kaufman. *Music:* Leonard Bernstein. *Design:*

Richard Day (a.d.). *Editing:* Gene Milford. *Production:* Sam Spiegel, Horizon Pictures, Columbia. 108 mn. Eight Oscars: best film, direction, screenplay, photography, artistic direction, editing, best actor (Marlon Brando), best supporting actress (Eva Marie Saint). *Cast:* Marlon Brando, (Terry Malloy), Eva Marie Saint (Eddie Doyle) Lee J. Cobb (Johnny Friendly), Karl Malden (Father Barry), Rod Steiger (Charley Malloy), Pat Henning ("Kayo" Dugan), Leif Erickson (Glover), Arthur Keegan (Jimmy), James Westerfield (Big Mac), Tony Galento (Truck), Tami Mauriello (Tillio), John Hamilton ("Pop" Doyle), John Helderbrand (Mutt), Rudy Bond (Moose), Don Blackman (Luke), Abe Simon (Barney), Barry McCollum (J.P.), Mike O'Dowd (Specs), Martin Balsam (Gillette), Fred Gwynne (Slim), Ann Hegira (Mrs Collins), Thomas Hanley (Tommy), Joyce Leal.

1954 EAST OF EDEN

Screenplay: Paul Osborn, after the novel by John Steinbeck. *Photography:* Ted McCord (Cinemascope, Warnercolor). *Music:* Leonard Rosenman. *Design:* James Basevi, Malcolm Bert (a.d), George James Hopkins (s.d.). *Editing:* Owen Marks. *Costumes:* Anna Hill Johnstone. *Production:* Elia Kazan, Warner Bros. 115 mn. Oscar for Jo Van Fleet (best supporting actress). *Cast:* Julie Harris (Abram), James Dean (Cal Trask), Raymond Massey (Adam Trask), Richard Davalos (Aron Trask), Jo Van Fleet (Kate), Burl Ives (Sheriff Sam Cooper), Albert Dekker (Will Hamilton), Lois Smith (Ann), Harold Gordon (Mr Albrecht), Timothy Carey (Joe), Mario Siletti (Piscora), Lonny Chapman (Roy), Nick Dennis (Rantany).

1956 BABY DOLL

Screenplay: Tennessee Williams (in fact, Kazan's adaptation of two one-acters by Williams: *The Long Stay Cut Short, or The Unsatisfactory Meal* and *27 Wagons Full of Cotton*). *Photography:* Boris Kaufman. *Music:* Kenyon Hopkins. *Design:* Richard Sylbert, Paul Sylbert (a.d.). *Editing:* Gene Milford. *Costume:* Anna Hill Johnstone. *Production:* Newtown Productions (Elia Kazan), Warner Bros. 114 mn. *Cast:* Karl Malden (Archie Lee Meigham), Carroll Baker (Baby Doll), Eli Wallach (Silva Vacarro), Mildred Dunnock (Aunt Rose Comfort), Lonny Chapman (Rock), Eades Hogue (the marshal), Noah Williamson (the mayor), John S. Dudley (the doctor), Madeleine Sherwood (nurse), Will Lester (sheriff).

1956 A FACE IN THE CROWD

Screenplay: Budd Schulberg, after his short story "Your Arkansas Traveler" in the collection *Some Faces in the Crowd*. *Photography:* Harry Stradling, Gayne Rescher. *Music:* Tom Glazer. *Songs:*

Tom Glazer, Budd Schulberg. *Design:* Richard Sylbert, Paul Sylbert (a.d.). *Costumes:* Anna Hill Johnstone. *Editing:* Gene Milford. *Production:* Newtown Productions (Elia Kazan), Warner Bros. 126 mn. *Cast:* Andy Griffith (Lonesome Rhodes), Patricia Neal (Marcia Jeffries), Anthony Franciosa (Joey De Palma), Walter Matthau (Mel Miller), Lee Remick (Betty Lou Fleckum), Percy Waram (Colonel Hollister), Rod Brasfield (Beanie), Charles Irving (Mr Luffler), Howard Smith (J.B. Jeffries), Paul McGrath (Macey), Kay Medford (the first Mrs Rhodes), Alexander Kirkland (Jim Collier), Marshal "Mickey" Neilan (Senator Fuller), Big Jeff Bess (Sheriff Hosmer), Henry Sharp (Abe Steiner), P. Jay Sidney (Llewellyn), Eva Vaughan (Mrs Cooley).

1960 WILD RIVER
Screenplay: Paul Osborn, after the novels *Mud on the Stars* by William Bradford Huie and *Dunbar's Cove* by Borden Deal. *Photography:* Ellsworth Fredericks (Scope, De Luxe). *Music:* Kenyon Hopkins. *Design:* Lyle R. Wheeler, Herman R. Blumenthal (a.d.), Walter M. Scott, Joseph Kish (s.d.). *Editing:* William Reynolds. *Production:* Elia Kazan, Twentieth-Century Fox. 110mn. *Cast:* Montgomery Clift (Chuck Glover), Lee Remick (Carol), Jo Van Fleet (Ella Garth), Albert Salmi (Hank Bailey), Jay C. Flippen (Hamilton Garth), James Westerfield (Cal Garth), Barbara Loden (Betty Jackson), Frank Overton (Walter Clark), Malcolm Atterbury (Sy Moore), Robert Earl Jones (Ben), Bruce Dern (Jack Roper), James Steakley (Mayor Maynard), Hardwick Stuart (Marshal Hogue).

1960 SPLENDOR IN THE GRASS
Screenplay: William Inge. *Photography:* Boris Kaufman (Technicolor). *Music:* David Amram. *Design:* Richard Sylbert. *Editing:* Gene Milford. *Costumes:* Anna Hill Johnstone. *Choreography:* George Tapps. *Ass. Prod.:* William Inge, Charles H. Maguire. An Elia Kazan Production, Newton NBI Production. *Dist.:* Warner Bros. 124 mn. *Cast:* Natalie Wood (Wilma Dean "Deannie" Loomis), Warren Beatty (Bud Stamper), Pat Hingle (Ace Stamper), Audrey Christie (Mrs Loomis), Barbara Loden (Ginny Stamper), Zohra Lampert (Angelina), Fred Stewart (Del Loomis), Joanna Roos (Mrs Stamper), Jan Norris (Juanita Howard), Gary Lockwood (Toots), Sandy Dennis (Kay), Crystal Field (Hazel), Marla Adams (June), Lynn Loring (Carolyn), John McGovern (Doc. Smiley), Martine Bartlett (Miss Metcalf), Charles Robinson (Johnny Masterson), Sean Garrison (Glenn), William Inge (Reverend Whiteman), Phyllis Diller (Texas Guinan), Buster Bailey (old man at the Country Club), Jake La Motta (man with oysters), Billy Graham, Charlie Norkus (youths who fight with Bud in the parking lot).

1964 AMERICA AMERICA
Screenplay: Elia Kazan, after his novel *America America*. *Photography:* Haskell Wexler. *Music:* Manos Hadjidakis. *Lyrics:* Nikos Gatsos. *Design:* Gene Callahan. *Editing:* Dede Allen. *Costumes:* Anna Hill Johnstone. *Production:* Elia Kazan, Warner Bros. 168 mn. *Cast:* Stathis Giallelis (Stavros Topouzoglou), Frank Wolff (Vartan Damadian), Harry Davis (Isaac Topouzoglou), Elena Karam (Vasso Topouzoglou), Estelle Hemsley (the grandmother), Gregory Rozakis (Hohannes Gardashian), Lou Antonio (Abdul), Salem Ludwig (Odysseus Topouzoglou), John Marley (Garabet), Joanna Frank (Vartuhi), Linda Marsh (Thomna Sinnikoglou), Paul Mann (Aleko Sinnikoglou), Robert H. Harris (Aratoon Kebabian), Katharine Balfour (Sophia Kebabian).

1969 THE ARRANGEMENT
Screenplay: Elia Kazan after his novel of the same name. *Dir. photo:* Robert Surtees (Technicolor). *Editing:* Stefan Arnsten. *Design:* Gene Callahan. *Art. Dir.:* Malcolm Bert. *Music:* David Amram. *Costumes:* Theodore Van Runkle. *Sound:* Richard Vorisek. *Sound Editing:* Larry Jost. *Production:* Elia Kazan. *Production Company:* Athena Enterprises. *Ass. prod.:* Charles H. Maguire. *Dist.:* Warner Bros. 125 mn. *Assist.:* Burtt Harris. *Cast:* Kirk Douglas (Eddie Anderson), Faye Dunaway (Gwen), Deborah Kerr (Florence Anderson), Richard Boone (Sam Anderson), Hume Cronyn (Arthur), Michael Higgins (Michael), John Randolph Jones (Charles), Carol Rossen (Gloria), Anne Hegira (Thomna), William Hansen (Dr Weeks), Charles Drake (Finnegan), Harold Gould (Dr Liebman), E. J. André (Uncle Joe), Michael Murphy (old Draddy), Philip Bourneuf (Judge Morris), Diane Hull (Ellen), Barry Sullivan (chief Collier), Anne Doran (nurse Costello), chief Stratton (Charlie), Paul Newlan (banker), Steve Bond (Eddie at twelve), Jim Rafferty (Eddy at eighteen).

1971 THE VISITORS
Production: Chris Kazan, Nick Proferes. *Production company:* Home Free. *Dist.:* United Artists. 90 mn. *Screenplay:* Chris Kazan. *Photography:* Nick Proferes (super 16, color). *Lighting:* Michael L. Mannes. *Lighting assist.:* William Mamches. *Editing:* Nick Proferes. *Music:* Bach's Suite No. 1 played on the guitar by William Matthews. *Sound editing:* Nina Shulman. *Sound mix:* Richard Vorisek. *Sound:* Dale Whitman. *Sound editing assist.:* Marilyn Frauenglass. *Cast:* Patrick McVey (Harry Wayne), Patricia Joyce (Martha Wayne), James Woods (Bill Schmidt), Chico Martinez (Tony Rodriguez), Steve Railsback (Mike Nickerson).

1976 THE LAST TYCOON
Production: Sam Spiegel. A Sam Spiegel–Elia Kazan production. *Prod. Manager:* Lloyd Anderson. *Dist.:* Paramount 122 mn. *Screenplay:* Harold Pinter, after the novel by F. Scott Fitzgerald. *Dir. photo:* Victor Kemper (Panavision, Technicolor). *Cameraman:* Richard Bruno; *assts:* Ray de la Motte, Ron Vargas. *Music:* Maurice Jarre. *Prod. Designer:* Gene Callahan. *Art Dir.:* Jack Collis. *Set dec.:* Jerry Wunderlich. *Set des.:* Billy Smith. *Editing:* Richard Marks; *asst:* Hanna Wajshonig. *Costumes:* Anna Hill Johnstone, Anthea Sylbert. *Spec. Eff.:* Henry Millar. *Sound:* Larry Jost. *Asst dir.:* Danny McCauley. *2nd asst dirs:* Ron Wright, Gary Daigler. *Cast:* Robert De Niro (Monroe Stahr), Tony Curtis (Rodriguez), Robert Mitchum (Pat Brady), Jeanne Moreau (Didi), Jack Nicholson (Brimmer), Donald Pleasence (Boxley), Ingrid Boulting (Kathleen Moore), Ray Milland (Mort Fleishacker), Dana Andrews (Red Ridingwood), Theresa Russell (Cecilia Brady), Peter Strauss (Wylie White), Tige Andrews (Popolos), Morgan Farley (Marcus) John Carradine (guide), Jeff Corey (doctor), Diane Shalet (Stahr's secretary), Seymour Cassell (seal trainer), Angelica Houston (Edna), Bonnie Bartlett (Brady's first secretary), Sharon Masters (Brady's second secretary), Eric Christmas (Norman), Leslie Curtis (Mrs Rodriguez), Lloyd Kino (butler), Brendan Burns (assistant editor), Carrie Miller (woman in restaurant), Peggy Feury (hairdresser), Betsey Jones-Moreland (scriptwriter), Patricia Singer (girl on beach).

This filmography was compiled up until *America America* by Bernard Eisenschitz and Roger Tailleur for Roger Tailleur's book on Elia Kazan (Seghers, 1966).

ACKNOWLEDGEMENTS

We thank for their invaluable help Eileen Shanahan, Elia Kazan's secretary, the Museum of Modern Art (Mary Corliss) and the British Film Institute (Michèle Snappes, Markku Salmi).

PHOTO CREDITS

Frank D. Dandridge, *54/55, 210.*
Fred Fehl, *168.*
Henry Grossman, *cover photo, 236/237.*
Constantine Manos, *26/27, 56, 57, 225, 230.*
Sam Shaw, *24/25.*
W. Eugene Smith, *158.*
Marion Post Wolcott, *151, 156.*

Elia Kazan in the study of his West Side house in 1973.